JOYCE CARY:
A PREFACE TO HIS NOVELS

JOYCE CARY

JOYCE CARY:
A Preface to his Novels

Andrew Wright

*Associate Professor of English
at Ohio State University*

GREENWOOD PRESS, PUBLISHERS
WESTPORT, CONNECTICUT

The Library of Congress has catalogued this publication as follows:

Library of Congress Cataloging in Publication Data

Wright, Andrew H
  Joyce Cary: a preface to his novels.

  Reprint of the 1958 ed.
  Bibliography: p.
  1. Cary, Joyce, 1888-1957.
  [PR6005.A77Z8 1972]   823'.9'12   72-138602
  ISBN 0-8371-5804-4

Originally published in 1958 by Harper & Brothers,
New York

Reprinted with the permission of Harper & Row,
Publishers

Reprinted in 1972 by Greenwood Press, Inc.,
51 Riverside Avenue, Westport, Conn. 06880

Library of Congress catalog card number 72-138602
ISBN 0-8371-5804-4

Printed in the United States of America

10 9 8 7 6 5 4 3 2

FOR GINA AGAIN

Foreword

WHEN I went to Oxford in April of 1956 I hardly knew Joyce Cary. We had indeed met three years before, when he was in America on a lecture tour, and we had dined together twice. I admired his novels and liked him, but I had no idea then of writing a book about him. However, he remained in my mind as his books haunted my imagination; and a couple of years later I wrote him a letter asking whether he would allow me to undertake a work about him. Here is his reply:

I should be delighted and most flattered that you should write a book about me, and if you want any material or references I should be eager to give them. . . .

As for biographical facts, ask me anything you like. I don't mean to write an autobiography, but there is a certain amount of reminiscence in books like *A House of Children,* and the short story "Bush River" is an account of actual fact. . . .

A good time to begin as I've just finished the 2nd trilogy. Last volume comes out in April. . . .

From the very beginning, therefore—and even at long distance—our relationship was candid. I wrote him a good many letters in the year before I was able to go to Oxford, and he was always kind enough to reply fully, thoughtfully and frankly. What I was not prepared for was the unstinting generosity of his time and effort when I was seeing him every day in Oxford—not because I did not expect kindness, but because he was an extremely busy man. Nor of course did I know that we would become friends.

For nearly six months I went daily to his house in Parks Road. He gave me his study on the second floor to work in; he gave me permission to use anything I found. In the attic and in the study I found manuscripts of novels, short stories, essays, plays, poems, journals, letters. I found bills, memoranda, wallets, pistols, medals, trunks, boxes and bicycle tires. I have made a good deal of use of the literary and biographical materials which turned up; that I was able to use them freely is, I understand, not only unusual but almost unique: most people conceal or with-hold some at least of the facts. Cary did not.

And Cary also talked to me with entire candour about himself and his work. As I came to know him well, I came to have a sense of the personality behind his novels, and this is, I think, a good sense to have. But he was an artist and not always, about his own works, a critic. In *Herself Surprised*, Matthew Monday says to Gulley Jimson about one of his paintings, 'I think I see what you mean.' Gulley's reply is, 'It's more than I do.' Furthermore, the works Cary had written long ago he had got out of his system, and had actually forgotten about a good many of them: it was I who told him about them rather than the other way round. There were certain questions which Cary could not answer because he did not know what the answers were, or else he had forgotten them. But from him I learned in a general way how to read his works better, and I hope this book records clearly the insights which he taught me to look for.

A word more. Joyce Cary was a generous and lively man who gave and responded to affection. In the last year of his life, when he was crippled by muscular atrophy and fully aware of the imminence of his own death, he remained vigorous in spirit. Like Gulley Jimson he kept on keeping on, not to ward off despair but because he had a lot to do. We became friends, and I shall always think of knowing Joyce Cary as one of the luckiest and best things that has happened to me. But that is only half the story. Affection for the man and understanding of his work have grown out of one another. Affection and criticism are themselves on friendly terms. That is what I learned in Oxford last year, and I am very glad of it.

Worthington, Ohio
December 1957

Acknowledgments

AMONG the best criticism of Joyce Cary is that by Cary himself in the essays listed in the bibliography. I have drawn heavily on these. I have drawn heavily also on the excellent essays of Walter Allen, David Craig, Glenn Hatfield, Pamela Hansford Johnson, Arnold Kettle and J. Maclaren Ross: these essays are also listed in the bibliography.

The American Philosophical Society for the Promotion of Useful Knowledge provided me with a grant by which I travelled to England during what turned out to be the last year of Cary's life. I am profoundly grateful.

Ruth Hein and Elizabeth Lawrence gave me access to the Cary files at Harper's in New York; Jeremy Hadfield and the late Michael Joseph were equally kind in London; and Peter Janson-Smith was good enough to help me with the translations. Arnold Chandler, Clarene Dorsey, Ruth Erlandson and Sidney E. Matthews all provided me with bibliographical assistance.

Cary's friends and relations have been of great help. Lionel Stevenson, Cary's cousin, sent me copies of Cary's early poems. Edith Millen, Cary's secretary, has been endlessly patient and kind. All the Dan Davin family have turned to with an enthusiasm that reflects not only deep affection for Cary but also a natural kindness. I should like to mention Anna Davin especially, who frequently led me to the manuscripts and helped me search among them. Helen Gardner showed me the notes of her California lecture on Cary; these are of the outstanding quality which has come to be taken for granted from this superbly learned and sensitive scholar.

Robert Shedd has read the first half of this book in manuscript, and Robert Estrich and Roy Harvey Pearce have read it all; these friends have made possible many improvements in focus, emphasis and style. Another friend, M. O. Percival, has contributed greatly to the possible value of this book by his glosses of the Blake quotations in *The Horse's Mouth*. What remains in the way of wrongheadedness is not theirs but mine.

The help of Gill and Bill Williams, though somewhat less direct than that acknowledged in the foregoing paragraphs, has been altogether specific and altogether nourishing.

A. W.

Contents

CHAPTER ONE

Background

"AS a routine production, as an exploitable mine, the novel may be finished," writes Ortega y Gasset in his tantalizing *Notes on the Novel*. "The large veins, accessible to any diligent hand, are worked out." Indeed, a catalogue of past achievement is equally, no doubt, a catalogue of future limitation. Henry James's "commanding centre," Conrad's invention of Marlow, James Joyce's war with time, D. H. Lawrence's conspiratorial intimacy, and Hemingway's formal objectivity of viewpoint—to speak but of the recent past—all these novelistic inventions or refinements do without question circumscribe as well as liberate other novelists. The novel has developed, and although it is still the loosest of all the literary modes it has now so many precedents that the writer must attend to them. "What remains," Ortega says, "are hidden deposits and perilous ventures into the depths where, perhaps, the most precious crystals grow. But that is work for minds of rare distinction."

And the originality of Joyce Cary lies, it seems to me, not in his discovery of new mines, but in re-exploration of the old ones. No mere list can do justice to his novelistic energy. The Smollettesque dialogue, the Shandean capital letters, the Dickensian names, the brackets (and brackets within brackets), the historical present tense, the abrupt chapter divisions, above all the picaresque structure—these are but a few of the styles which Cary has rehabilitated and reshaped for his own purposes. In the two trilogies, furthermore, he has achieved a multiplicity of viewpoint quite new

to the novel, although this invention involves a reordering
of one of the oldest of fictional artifices, narration in the
first person. And I should say that the fact of Cary's great
versatility both substantiates Ortega's generalization
about the novel in the present day and underscores Cary's
anxiety to achieve in his novels a marriage between intuition and form. For technique, by itself, is unimportant; it
is what is realized in and through technique that counts. It
is the work of art that counts. And Cary mastered his craft
not for virtuosity's sake but in urgency and profound
concern. The function of the novel is nothing less, he writes,
than "to make the world contemplate and understand itself,
not only as rational being but as experience of value, as a
complete thing."

Each of Cary's novels has behind it notebooks filled with
samples of dialogue, sketches of situations, statements of
idea; each of the works has its dossier, a collection of notes
toward the novel; each of the novels has its false beginnings, its rejected chapters. In an appendix to this book
there are samples of some of this vast preliminary work;
and "The Old Strife at Plant's," first published in *Harper's*
magazine, is a chapter of *The Horse's Mouth* which, before
it was finally incorporated into the book, was drastically
reshaped. "I do not write," he says in "My First Novel,"
"and never have written, to an arranged plot. The book is
composed over the whole surface at once like a picture,
and may start anywhere, in the middle or at the end. I may
go from the end to the beginning on the same day, and
then from the beginning to the middle. As in picture com-
position, this involves continual trial and error and a lot
of waste. Whole chapters get moved from one place to
another, or perhaps thrown out altogether; characters
appear and disappear. I should think I write about three

times the material that finally appears in any book, that is to say, for a novel of about 100,000 words I write at least 300,000. This is of course a fearful waste, and I have tried to avoid it, but it seems to me the only way in which I can get the kind of form I want, a certain balance and unity within a given context." In Cary's work there is, in short, exploration of old territory, discovery of new possibilities, creation—sometimes in desperation and always out of the old materials—of new techniques.

But where, in his novels, does the meaning lie? Whose side is he on? In the African novels is he anti-colonial and pro-African, or something more disturbing? Are we to admire the childish Mister Johnson, who commits a murder in order to nourish his idea of himself as a black man bearing the white man's burden? In the same novel are we to admire Rudbeck, the colonial officer who wants to build a road simply because it was the first idea put into his head by a superior? What, furthermore, is the meaning of the first trilogy? Who is the real Sara Monday—the pious and eternally penitent woman of the self-portrait in *Herself Surprised*? Or the devoted housekeeper and mistress, the possessor of natural grace, whom Wilcher depicts in *To be a Pilgrim*? Or the predatory female drawn by Jimson in *The Horse's Mouth*? Is Cary championing the conservatism of Wilcher, or is he defending the anarchism of Jimson? Of the second trilogy the same kinds of questions can be asked. Who is the real Chester Nimmo—the man as seen by his wife, or by himself, or by his rival Jim Latter?

The difficulty here is one which Cary himself recognized. "My work does not," he said in a letter, "reveal any subjective centre. It deals as far as I can manage it with the whole landscape of existence; and though that landscape is seen from one point of view, the especial nature of the

15

point of view does not appear in the books." In fact, I think, because of the very success of his method he is liable to misinterpretation. But the landscape exists, and must be explored. Cary's novels have proceeded from a single and steady perception of the world's shape; although his art has developed, his work considered altogether remains remarkably consistent, faithful to the original intuition. And beyond the mirages of contemporaneity lie the fifteen novels themselves, bearing witness to the character of our time. They mirror the wisdom and folly, the strength and fragility, the hope and lament, the pity and cruelty—the disaster, joy, crisis, fulfilment and tragedy—which make up the complicated life of the complicated twentieth-century man. If like Dr Rieux at the end of Camus' *La Peste* Cary found more in men to admire than to despise, that is not because he made some compromise in the course of his journey: it is because, like Camus' hero, he saw in the eternal renewal of innocence, in the everlasting impulse to create, not defeated triumph, but the triumph of defeat.

Joyce Cary was born in Londonderry on December 7th, 1888, and christened Arthur Joyce Lunel. He was the first-born of Arthur Pitt Cary and of Charlotte Cary, *née* Joyce; he is a direct descendant of a George Cary who, having migrated to Ireland from Devon in the early part of the seventeenth century, became the first Recorder of London-derry and the first Member of Parliament for Londonderry in 1613. The Carys are a family with roots deep in Devon-shire, and with branches in America as well as in Ireland. "As a family," writes Fairfax Harrison, perhaps some-what romantically, in *The Devon Carys*, "they are remark-able for iterated loyalties to lost causes . . . Richard II, Henry VI, Charles I, and the Stuart Pretenders." But the Irish branch flourished for three centuries, owning for many generations the properties of Castle Cary, Red Castle and White Castle, of which they were resident landlords, until they were ruined at last by the land acts of the 1880s.

Although Joyce Cary was born in Ireland, his mother and father lived in London, first at Nunhead, later in the Kitto Road, where Charlotte Cary died in 1897. Joyce Cary's father, trained as an engineer, was a consultant to the Indian State Railways, and the first Cary for generations to follow a profession. But the Carys frequently returned to Ireland, and Joyce Cary wrote for the New York *Herald-Tribune* this recollection of the visits. "I had two different beings; with grandmother Cary, at Clare on the shores of Lough Foyle, I was often the only child. But the house was full of old portraits and old books. I read enormously and dreamed still more. From Clare I would wander in the old walled gardens of Castle Cary, with all the appropriate feelings of the banished heir in the romances. And the country people, with the Irish love of children and old tales, would tell me stories of my people. But at my grandmother Joyce's, at some holiday house taken for all her grandchildren, I would range over the countryside with a horde of cousins. We went fishing, exploring, stealing rides on other people's horses, sailing on the lough, often for long journeys. We were as free as the mountain slopes, and often in mischief."

Another source of childhood recollections is the auto-biographical novel, *A House of Children*, which, though it is discussed subsequently, must be touched on here. "Names, places and people are disguised, because many of the people are living," he writes in the preface to the Carfax edition. "I have given myself an elder brother— why I do not know. But I notice that this elder brother is also myself, and I suspect that I divided myself in this way

17

because I realized by some instinct (it was certainly not by reason) that the two together as a single character would be too complex for the kind of book I needed to write." That is, the book is true to intuition, rather than simply true to fact.

The impression is colourful and therefore not without shadow. Cary, who calls himself Evelyn Corner in the book, is a small boy of eight in a house of children, each of whom is discovering the world's shape: Evelyn and a boy called Red Cheeks putting snow and water down the kitchen chimney to see what will happen, and thus spectacularly ruining a holiday meal; the children off on night bathes, to experience the water in the darkness, to discover intimacy and terror; all of them developing in different directions, becoming uniquely themselves. There is Pinto, the holiday tutor, out for a sail with the children, saying, 'I suppose the fish take us for a bird.' There is old Roe, the gardener, who talks gloomily of hell-fire. There is Owney, his sixteen-year-old nephew, a boy with blackened teeth and a prison record, whose serenity derives from acceptance of life. There is Uncle James Foley, who lives for sport. And there is Evelyn's father, vigorous and skilful, who dives from a height of twenty feet into the harbour, making in the child's mind an ineradicable picture of grace.

Two experiences of art shape the young Evelyn's life. The first is an enormously complicated and serious play written by Evelyn's older brother Harry. Its theme, enunciated in long speeches by the two brothers, is "the glory of dying for freedom." Harry plays the parts of a king, a prime minister and a general; Evelyn, the part of an admiral. But the play is a disaster. The speeches are forgotten or muddled, the costumes are in confusion, the curtain catches fire. The children are beyond consolation, for they know how profoundly they have failed. "We were not only ashamed and disappointed; we had suffered a shock. Deeper than the sense of failure, there was the feeling that we had misunderstood the situation; that plays were not so easy as they seemed. With this went, as always, the feeling that life, too, was not so easy as it seemed." But the other experience provides a happier revelation. This occurs at an amateur production of *The Tempest*, when the young Evelyn begins to understand for the first time the force, the feeling, the meaning of poetry: the impact of the aesthetic experience. "Not only words for feelings, like beauty, love, hate, had taken life and meaning for me; but also concrete substances like mountain, sea, thunder, star, boat, began to have new significances. Of his bones are coral made; it was a chord of strings; a sextet, each singing quietly in the ear of my soul; not only with music but souls of their own."

The first chapter of Joyce Cary's life came abruptly to an end when he was eight. His mother died, and his father not long afterwards moved to Gunnersbury, near London, where the Tristram Carys—Joyce Cary's uncle and aunt—lived. Their house became the family centre. The young boy, though he still spent summer holidays with one or other of his grandmothers in Ireland, came to regard England as his home. He lived in an atmosphere, he says in "Cromwell House," of crisis: "crisis natural to a generation ruined in a land war, the cruellest, most tragic and unjust form of civil strife. For it is precisely those resident landlords, who have been born in the country, who lived and worked all their lives in it and put all their capital into it, who suffer most. To us from earliest childhood, in England or Ireland, the fundamental injustice of things, the cruelty of blind fate, was as natural as the air we breathed, and, as I think now, probably as important to our health. Cromwell House and the Irish households of my various relations had a sense of life, both older and more modern than that of our English cousins. We lived more intensely, and we set a far higher value on what we had of secure happiness. We were more eager in our attachments. We knew, more consciously than other children, what family affection meant, as the one trustworthy thing among so many treacheries."

Cary went to a preparatory school called Hurstleigh in Tunbridge Wells and from there to Clifton College. His school days, though not by any means gloriously happy, were not scarring. Indeed he had a measure of saving success. For though when he first went to Clifton he was, he has said, among a crowd of toughs and rather unhappy, he was a determined athlete; and, despite his slight stature, he was promoted to the house football team. From that moment school was tolerable. Nor did he confine himself to the playing field. In *The Cliftonian* for 1906 appears his first publication, an anonymous poem which stands out not on account of any special merit but because of its subject-matter. While his schoolmates were writing tetrameter verses "To My Pen" and in praise of Clifton ("The Lady of Our Love: A Song of Clifton"), Cary's thoughts were of Adam and Eve, his expression thirty-five lines of blank verse.

> *And he did ope his smiling eyes and look,*
> *Rose swift and clipt her soft snow-breast to his*
> *And lingering prest his warm red lips against*
> *Her soft flushed cheek, and all their eyes were wet;*
> *And so he took her by the hand—they passed,*
> *Two children in the garden of sweet peace.*

BACKGROUND

When he was seventeen, Cary left Clifton, intending to become a painter. According to *Time*, an artist had admired some water-colours he had done while on holiday in Étaples and "I thought, this is a damn good show. I was fed up with school and thought that the life of an artist would be a good life." He had a small private income—varying between £200 and £300 a year—from the Joyce side of the family; and, after staying for some months in Paris, he went to the Art School at the University of Edinburgh, where he remained for three years, though he frequently visited Paris in the meantime.

But at last, dissatisfied with his painting, he went up to Trinity College, Oxford. "I imagine now," he says in an unpublished autobiographical sketch, "that I was bored with art because I was more interested in people and ideas, but I daresay that another strong motive was the rootlessness and restlessness of a boy uprooted from the long romantic tradition of a family domain." At Oxford he read law and took a fourth-class honours degree, and there his life began to take mature shape. "What I worked at was friendship, a vast reading and much talk, especially on ethics and philosophy." John Middleton Murry, a close friend with whom Cary later shared lodgings in Paris and Oxford, wrote this recollection in "Coming to London": "Joyce Cary was one of a group of Trinity men, whom I found very attractive. They were a little older than the average undergraduate . . . something had intervened for them between the public school and the university, which made the difference. They were neither overgrown sixth-form boys, like me, nor pass-men up for a good time. There was nothing precious about them, yet their intellectual interests were various and widespread; and they

21

judged for themselves. To me they were vastly stimu-
lating."

Among such friends and in this atmosphere Cary's
religious intuition became articulate. Up to a point his
religious history is conventionally that of a person born
in Victoria's reign and brought up within the Establishment. As a very young child he said his prayers to his
mother; as a boy at Hurstleigh he was deeply affected by
the testimonies of a militant missionary; at Clifton College
he was confirmed; before he was twenty he had abandoned
his faith, as he thought, forever. It was not until he went
up to Oxford that Cary, trying to make sense of the world
as he experienced it, went beyond this youthful scepticism
to the roots of the faith of which he later wrote. At Oxford
he read Kant and Blake, but Blake especially, who, he
writes in an unpublished essay, "introduced me into a
highly complex universe where what is called the material
is entirely dissolved into imaginative construction and
states of feeling, where matter, mind and emotion, become
simply different aspects of one reality." Blake thus
provided the beginnings of an answer to the problems
posed by the dualities of good and evil, love and hate,
spirit and substance, intuition and expression. Cary's
religion, focused by the Protestant tradition, sharpened by
the enthusiasm of the evangelical movement, conditioned
by his time, lost in youth and found in manhood—Cary's
religion owed much to Blake, whom he read as a poet and
looked at as an artist. For, "it was almost entirely through
the aesthetic experience that I came to a true faith." But
not at once. And from Oxford, now bent on becoming a
writer, he went to Paris briefly with Middleton Murry.
There they shared lodgings, poverty and a sense of dedica-
tion to art.

BACKGROUND

In his unpublished Paris journal Cary records something of his life there. This entry is typical:

"Jan. 2nd [1911]. Bad dreams from chestnuts. Felt as if there were a frozen stake through me, and can remember comparing my sensation to that of a suicide at the cross-roads. Nor could I wake up for a long while. Got up at 12. To the Avenue de l'Opéra to change money at Cooks....

"Slept and worked by turns in the afternoon, and slept from 5 till 6.30 as I did not want to pay for another meal, or I shall have nothing for the evening. Talk and friends, after all, are more necessary than three meals a day. Indeed, in Bohemia, than any meals, for with no talk, no ideas, and with no ideas, no work, and with no work neither happiness nor meals. To dinner, soupe, chateau jardiniere, and tarte noisette. Back again very lazy—(saw the Pirate with a rich looking catch on the way. She does catch well, she has a buccaneering way that is not to be escaped.)"

Back in Oxford, Cary again shared lodgings with Middleton Murry, who was discovering Katherine Mansfield by way of *Rhythm*, to which she sent contributions. In this period Cary undertook a novel about student life in Paris, and he also, Middleton Murry recalls, "covered the sitting-room floor with foolscap sheets of Caroline lyrics—about eight lines to the page; which was extravagant of paper but gave him a necessary feeling of elbow-room. For the same reason, I suppose, he did most of his writing on the floor, with an exceptionally blunt quill pen." But toward the end of this year the Balkan War of 1912-13 broke out, and Cary went to it. "I wanted the experience of war," he says. "I thought there would be no more wars. And I had a certain romantic enthusiasm for the cause of the Montenegrins; in short I was young and eager for any

23

sort of adventure." The adventure is brilliantly recorded in the unpublished *Memoir of the Bobotes.*

He intended to join the Montenegrin army, but while he was exploring the Venetian fortress of Antivari, it blew up, and he was arrested as a spy. From this predicament he was rescued by Captain Martin Leake, V.C., whom he helped with the wounded and whose Red Cross unit he joined at the front. "I saw most of the fighting," he writes, "and was among the first three over Scutari bridge, at the surrender of the Turks in 1913. For this campaign I had a little gold medal [the equivalent of the Military Cross] from the Montenegrin government which I prize very much, though it was earned in what was, for a boy of my age, a holiday."

Cary next spent a brief period as a member of Sir Horace Plunkett's Co-operative Society in Ireland. "My idea," he says, "was to do something useful and practical for the Irish peasantry, and perhaps find time and material for writing. Plunkett's idea was to use members of old Anglo-Irish families like myself in this work, because of their supposed special sympathy and influence with the people. But I found very soon that other members of the Co-operative organization had different views. They wanted agricultural specialists, and probably they were right." So, after a few months, he resigned from this job and joined the Nigerian service. "I wanted to see primitive Africa and I was attracted, as to the Irish job, by the chance of what seemed to me important and valuable constructive political work. For I still had a disgust for all the emotional and bitter political feeling which had surrounded my childhood."

Africa, where he remained for half a dozen years, was a crucial experience in Joyce Cary's life, a fact which many of his writings eloquently record. Part of the time he was a political officer—"magistrate, road builder, a general Pooh Bah of state"—and part of the time he was a soldier, serving in the 1915-16 Cameroons campaign, during which he was wounded at Mora mountain. After this campaign he returned to the political service, and for a year lived alone as District Office in the outpost of Borgu. He was invalided out of the service in 1920. A view of the young Cary in Africa is contained in the short story, "Bush River," which, he told me, is an account of actual fact. The principal is Captain Corner, "an extremely conventional young officer, a little bit of a dandy, a good deal of a cox-comb," who determines to swim Satan, a Barbary stallion, across a river against the manifest wishes of his soldiers. When Satan and he have successfully manœuvred this dangerous passage, Corner—who has enjoyed the terror of the crossing—is exultant; he has the feeling "of one appointed by chance to a special good fortune, to gratitude, to the accidents of fate." This story celebrates physical competence and fitness; it is an adventure story in which the adventure is self-justifying.

In 1916 Cary married Gertrude Ogilvie, and, each having a small private income, they settled in Oxford in 1920. There were four sons of the marriage. Michael, the eldest, took a first-class degree at Trinity College, Oxford, and he is now serving in the Diplomatic Corps in Paris. Peter, the second son, took his degree in English and lives in London. Tristram, the third son, is a composer. George, the youngest, a classical scholar and Fellow of Trinity College, Cambridge, died of a congenital heart ailment in January 1953 at the age of twenty-five. His book, *The Medieval Alexander*, was published posthumously in 1956.

Although it is true that Joyce Cary's career as a writer

really began in 1920, he had from his undergraduate days
determined to write; and, besides the work already
alluded to, he produced ten short stories during his African
service and sold them to the *Saturday Evening Post*, where
they were published under the pseudonym of Thomas
Joyce. These stories, though on the whole undistinguished,
display an inventiveness that, at least in retrospect, looks
promising; and one of them, interestingly enough, is pure
Conrad. But Cary was impatient. He thought the stories
trivial in theme, and when he wrote more ambitiously the
Saturday Evening Post complained. So ended his connection with that magazine.

From 1920 until 1932 Cary published nothing. "As soon
as I had finished a book," he has written of this period, "or
even if half finished it, I could not bear it. The truth was,
as I see now, that I was still an imitative writer. I had a
genuine desire to create, in writing, but had not yet found
an idea of life satisfying to myself. I was in short still
educating myself, and this process in Oxford went on much
more vigorously than in Africa." But no mere description,
not even Cary's own, can do justice to the silence of these
dozen years. Cary had the loyal and loving support of
his wife and family; he had also a wide circle of friends
"But," he said in conversation, "they did not know, they
could not know, what answers I sought, for I could not
formulate the questions." Toward the end of this period,
however, he began to see the world in what was for
him its true shape. And now he could write. *Aissa Saved*,
his first published novel, took him three years to finish,
but he finished it. "After that," he says, "I wrote easily
and quickly."

During the Second World War, Cary served on Civil
Defence in Oxford. In 1943 he went to East Africa, where

he assisted, as political adviser, in the production of a film called *Men of Two Worlds*. In 1946 he went to India in a similar capacity. "This journey," he writes, "through India, of four months, meeting Indians of all classes and professions, was worth a lifetime of mere reflection in a study. To see not only an empire, but a government, in dissolution; to see the dilemma of those who demanded freedom but were terrified of it; to see above all the help-lessness of the great mass of men and even their leaders in the grip of forces which had passed beyond the control of any authority; to see the historic tragedy played on such a great and naked stage, was an experience that gives deeper knowledge than history books, and precisely that know-ledge which is needed to make modern history compre-hensible outside the books. From this journey, as from the others, I went back to my Oxford study, and a very retired life, not because I don't like company, but because I have a lot of work to do. Besides, I have always been a family man, and as every family man knows, family duties take up much time."

After the death of his wife in 1949, Cary made two extensive American lecture tours, as well as several tours to Europe. In January of 1955, having embarked in an aeroplane for a lecture in Greece, he was in a serious accident. In taking off, the aeroplane crashed into a fence. Fortunately, the aeroplane did not catch fire, and the passengers were only shaken up; characteristically, Cary took the next flight to Rome. But from the spring of that year he suffered increasingly from a progressive muscular atrophy. He continued to write. The Clark Lectures for 1956 he completed in August of that year, and he had nearly finished a new novel, *The Captive and the Free*, before his death on March 29th, 1957.

CHAPTER TWO

Theme: The Politics of Freedom

1 *Freedom First*

"THE fundamental question," Cary insists in the Carfax preface to *The African Witch*, "the root of all politics, all arts, is what do men live by?" This is the question whose terms and conditions Cary had to work out for himself in the dozen years between his retirement as a political officer and the publication of his first novel. His answer, which is thoroughly English, constitutes, in varying degrees of fullness, the theme of all his novels. Cary's theme is that the answer derives from a consideration of freedom's shape and freedom's consequences. It stems both from the intuition of man's freedom and from the intuition of grace; but, and this also is English, the intuition is constantly tested and exemplified in that densely human experience which is the very stuff of the novel: the often splendid and often remarked paradox of English civilization altogether is that it is at once mystical and empirical, soaring and matter-of-fact.

Critics call Cary a traditional novelist, by which they mean that his work reveals an acquaintance with the work of other novelists, and also that he has not tried to go beyond James Joyce and Gertrude Stein in novelistic experiment. There is indeed in Cary's work the superb naturalness and superb zest of a Defoe. There is the generosity of a Fielding. There is occasionally the deliberate haphazard of Sterne's construction. There is the interest in character as grotesque which is a feature of the

novels of Smollett, Dickens and Surtees. There is Trollope's sturdy professionalism. And so on. But to draw
these comparisons is to reveal two things about them:
first, that some of them are judgments not about the novel
but about the English temperament; and second that to
find resemblances is not the same thing as to find identities.
For most English novels do not deal with fundamentally
existential questions; they are, at least until after Jane
Austen, manuals of behaviour. Moll Flanders knows that,
having refused to become a domestic, she must survive "by
my fingers' ends," and she enters upon her career of whore-
dom and thievery with a cheerful zest quite unmatched
elsewhere in the English novel. Moll knows that the world
turns on money and material possessions; she never questions this "fact": she simply accommodates herself to it.
Tom Jones knows and knows well what men live by: they
live by the gentlemanly precepts preached by Squire All-
worthy. Or rather, naturally good people learn at last to
live by these precepts; the naturally evil—the Blifils of the
world—can never escape from the devils with which they
are born, whatever they come to believe. Roderick Ran-
dom, for all his railings against the world, is, like Smollett
himself, a fundamentally conventional man. He knows
what men should live by; that they do not is a matter for
bitterness and sorrow.

Indeed, it is only in the nineteenth century that the
question begins to have something like a modern signi-
fication. It is only in the nineteenth century that novels
become metaphysical. But not at once. Scott, in romanticiz-
ing history, will domesticate the heroic ideals which he
finds exemplified in his nation's past. The hero of *Old
Mortality*, Henry Morton of Milnwood, learns, though
painfully, how to behave moderately in the face of the

fanaticism of seventeenth-century Scotland. Jane Austen's
novels all have a common tendency, toward a social centre
which is universally acknowledged to be central, which is
taken for granted in the sense that it is assumed to be
workable, possible, if imperfect. When Emma can learn
how to behave herself, when she fully discovers herself in
relation to the world of Hartfield and Highbury, she
deserves, and gets, Mr Knightley. The works of Dickens,
Thackeray and Trollope reveal deep fissures in the landscape of belief; but all three of these writers were bound,
though in varying degrees and different ways, to a shape
of belief that was simply assumed. *Hard Times* is a corus-
cating indictment of the utilitarian denial, as Dickens
thinks, of man's true nature. But, in the terms of that book,
man's true nature is known; Gradgrind and even
Bounderby become pitiable figures because they have been
deluded about the nature of existence. Thackeray, in showing what the people of Vanity Fair live by, implies by his
altogether transparent irony—and by his depiction of
Amelia and Dobbin—what they should live by. Thackeray
himself is vexed that wickedness should be so fascinating
and goodness so dull, but he knows clearly what constitutes
the good life. Finally Trollope, who is surely the most
often underrated among the Victorian novelists, knows
that not all men live by standards of generosity and good-
heartedness, bravery and integrity; but these are the
values which he celebrates, and which he supposes to
constitute man at his best.

With George Eliot, Hardy and Conrad, the twentieth-
century sense of the question asserts itself; this is, of
course, why these writers seem modern and the others do
not. This also explains the special appeal of Tolstoy and
Dostoevsky to the twentieth century. The world of *Adam*

THEME: THE POLITICS OF FREEDOM

Bede is one of profound disharmony; the blossoming trees mock Hetty's despair. Hardy, with an anguish that is evident throughout the canon but which becomes rawer in his later novels, records the paltry and futile efforts of man to accommodate himself to the inexorable and indifferent rhythm of nature; Jude's fate was so horrible that Hardy had to abandon the writing of novels. And Conrad's novels are above all else metaphysical—metaphysical in a way specially appealing to Cary, who was, like Conrad, a man of action. Of all Conrad's works, surely "Heart of Darkness" poses most centrally the question which Cary asks. From Tolstoy and Dostoevsky Cary also learned much. He learned that they, like himself, were bedevilled by the nature of existence; he felt licensed by the extended colloquies in their novels to make his own works philosophical. *The Moonlight* is an answer to *The Kreutzer Sonata*, a work full of speculation about the nature of man; *The Brothers Karamazov* had a most powerful influence upon Cary because there Dostoevsky himself became in turn the various figures in the conflict. "Dostoevsky," Cary says in "Roman à Thèse," "did not create Ivan out of theories and theology; out of paper. He himself was Ivan. But he was also Zossima and Alyosha. . . . He knew them, he lived in them, and they carried his own passions, his own convictions; their conflict was his conflict."

Cary's attempt to come to terms with the terms of existence itself, makes him unmistakably modern—in the sense that Proust and Joyce and Mann are modern. I dare say that Cary could not have written *A House of Children* had he not read Proust. In a review of the American edition, Walter Allen remarks that "just as for Proust the taste of the *madeleine* dipped in lime-flower tea brings back remembrance of things past, so for Cary a sudden glimpse

31

of a branch of fuchsia evokes the image of 'dazzling sun-light on miles of crinkling water' and a flood of memories of childhood." From the very first page the route is through sensation—the sight of the fuchias and the smell of the breeze—to the imaginative reconstruction of the incident which the sensation evokes: "I was waiting for a sail, probably my first sail into the Atlantic. Somebody or something must have fixed that moment upon my dreaming senses, so that I still possess it. . . . That moment was grasped out of the flux; a piece of life, unique and eternal, and the sail also, is still my living delight." For Proust, however, this epistemology became the organizing principle of his art. For Cary it is a daring experiment, not fully satisfactory because it does not enable him to give adequate form to his own intuition.

Like Mann, Cary tried the chronicle form of the novel; unlike Mann, he tried it repeatedly and always, in my opinion, failed. No twentieth-century man can help being haunted by the sense of history, for it gives—or, we think, ought to give—the rationale of human existence. As Mann had the prescience to observe in *Buddenbrooks*, recurrence is deceptive. *Buddenbrooks* is about decline; so, indeed, is *Castle Corner*, which, Cary told me, was meant to end with the castle made into a boarding-house. But Cary, like Mann, was led by his intuition and his experience into other pathways. He discovered that though the good is forever being destroyed, it is also forever being reborn: every day is a new creation, of good and evil, but since it is an individual creation, a personal creation, it can best be expressed (or is by Cary anyway best expressed) in works centrally personal rather than historical. This is why *The Moonlight* and *A Fearful Joy* fail. Neither of them has a personal centre. And I suspect that Mann was able to achieve what seems to me his greatest success in *Felix Krull* because there, rehabilitating the picaresque form as Cary also rehabilitates it, he was able to deal best with his perplexities about the nature of man.

Of James Joyce it must at once be said that already *Ulysses* and *Finnegans Wake* are period pieces; already James Joyce, the greatest of all the twentieth-century novelists, belongs to the past. His style is no longer a discovery, for though it is not outmoded it is fixed; and another generation has come to deal freshly with the cultural materials that make the art of the novel. The range of James Joyce's unquiet imagination, the amplitude of his vision, above all the magnificent ordering in his work of deeply felt and altogether recognizable experience—these have permanently extended the boundaries of novelistic creation. But the Joycean revolution is over. It is won. And out of the wreckage there have emerged other novelists, among the foremost Joyce Cary.

These two Irishmen stand far apart. James Joyce, born to a middle-class family in decline, was Catholic and trained in Jesuit schools. He was an apostate, he was an exile, he was alone. Flying by the nets of Ireland only to be caught again and returned, in spirit at least, to his native land, James Joyce made his books out of the crumbling solidities of home, fatherland and Church; he recorded the dissolution of the nineteenth century and wrote its epitaph. Cary, on the other hand, was an Ulsterman, a member of an old Anglo-Irish family of resident landlords; he was Protestant and he was educated in England, which, though he was born in Ireland, was always his home. Cary did not publish his first novel until James Joyce's career and life were nearly finished; and Cary made his books out of a perception of eternal order, of character, behind the twentieth-century aspect of confusion and disorder. Nevertheless, as men of the twentieth century, both James Joyce and Joyce Cary were deeply concerned with the same question. "Joyce Cary's great subject," Helen Gardner said in a lecture in 1954, "is the human conscience, and his originality lies in his peculiar handling of the theme of conscience and his passionate interest in what governs and shapes a man's life, what are his imperatives and where lies the mainspring of his mechanism as a human being."

2 Political Writings

"I've been called a metaphysical novelist," Cary said in an interview in 1954, "and if that means I have a fairly clear and comprehensive idea of the world I'm writing about, I suppose that's true." Indeed, he has repeatedly insisted on the primacy of idea, of theme, in art. "In the final resort," he says in "Roman à Thèse", "all novel writing is moral. It is impossible to give form to a book without some moral creed. It may be confused, instinctive, founded on crude assumptions, but it must exist if only as a principle of choice. The writer is obliged to choose alternatives of word and action, and his only criterion is moral value." Although the configuration of Cary's landscape does, I think, become clear in the novels themselves, its shape can also be usefully explored by way of his other writings. For the political treatises, the poems, the short stories, certain fugitive pieces and the unpublished work all provide in simpler, sometimes in cruder, form insight into Cary's major concerns.

There are four political treatises: *Power in Men* (1939), *The Case for African Freedom* (1941, revised 1944),

THEME: THE POLITICS OF FREEDOM

Process of Real Freedom (1943) and *Britain and West Africa* (1946). Cary, who sometimes called himself a political scientist, and whose interest in politics reveals itself not only in these pamphlets but in the second trilogy and in a host of essays—Cary is deeply concerned with an idea of freedom that explains the injustice with which he was surrounded from childhood, and which is the normal and tragic lot of a man alive in any century. This concern is what threads together the political treatises.

Of these, the most interesting from the point of view of coming to understand the novels is *Power in Men*. Here Cary again and again rejects the nineteenth-century idea of freedom as absence of restraint. "A dead man," he writes, "feels the weight of no law. By the old notion of liberty he is the freest man in the world. In fact, he has no liberty at all." For the notion of liberty as absence of restraint is, he said recently, "merely an idea derived from freedom, the fundamental power which is always seeking to overcome restraint." His redefinition, in positive terms and with fifty years of experience behind him, is absolutely central to his idea of the world. Freedom is "creation in the act," he says. "It is therefore eternal and indestructible. Whether man recognizes it for what it is or calls it what it is not, it is always at work. The contempt and abuse of its enemies can no more destroy it than they can destroy being itself. It is and remains." This idea is dramatized with no doubt excessive insistence in *A Fearful Joy*, the heroine of which is repeatedly vitalized by the creative power of her scamp of a lover and husband, Dick Bonser. "In a world so profoundly creative," Cary writes in the Carfax preface to this novel, "what is not in creation withers away; and nothing, no church, no national idea or emblem, no institution, no political set-up, no human relation, can stay alive to the experience unless it be continually reborn and re-created to the imagination."

Cary thus does battle with the idea of progress. Marie Hasluck, the earnest newspaperwoman who gives *An American Visitor* its title, has been taught to believe in the idea of the noble savage, and thus to disdain the District Officer Bewsher and what he stands for. She is a pacifist. But savages, she discovers, do not behave nobly. Her world and her life are overturned. Cary, who was himself a District Officer in Nigeria, learned by direct experience that human beings do not always choose the good—not even the good as it is conceived by District Officers.

On the other hand, Cary's idea of freedom as a positive force, as something "real in the strictest and profoundest sense," does battle also, and even more obviously, with the deterministic notions of such otherwise disparate writers as Zola, Stephen Crane, Dreiser and even A. E. Housman. "Let us endure a while," writes Housman, "and see injustice done." But this invocation is impossible in Cary's thinking; nowhere in his work is there the presentation of man victimized by a mechanical and indifferent fate—the sort of presentation which is at the centre of Crane's "The Open Boat." For man is really free.

But if freedom is man's glory, it is also his tragedy. In fact, tragedy is inevitable as the outcome of the conflicts between man's free choices. Reconciliation is possible in the faith which realizes that these conflicts stem from the very freedom out of which the glories also proceed. So far as man's actions are concerned, reconciliation is possible in love and in art sometimes, but finally only in death—an Aissa being eaten alive by ants; a Mister Johnson being executed; a Gulley Jimson flung down from a condemned wall; a Chester Nimmo dead in a W.C.; a Jim Latter hanged. "Can anyone fail to suffer," Cary asks in an essay on his own method, "in the face of continued ruin of good men, good things, of all that is fine, true, delicate, in civilization built up over centuries by the devoted labour of generations? Can everyone console himself with the enjoyment of all that is fine, true, delicate, in the new arts, new aspirations which arise every day? It may not be possible to do so. We may be too old, too tired. We may be too lonely. Change may break our hearts." "This turmoil," Cary said in a broadcast, "is what we pay for being free creative souls."

Power in Men itself is a plea, not to acquiesce in the human tragedy but, by recognizing man for what he is, to shape government so that his impulse to freedom can be nourished. Cary is enunciating a liberal creed which has been reformed by the cruel facts of the twentieth century. He is building on the theological conception of moral freedom—essentially a power to act—a whole political theory. Writing at the end of the 1930s, he bitterly attacked nationalism as destructive of the free mind, for "it forbids a man to know any facts which deny the most ridiculous and worthless of creeds": he attacks also dictatorship as similarly destructive, because "all states that acknowledge no higher law than their own will and convenience" are enemies of freedom. The argument, he says, at the end, is "not that governments and peoples are morally bound to do certain things for the sake of" freedom, but that because freedom is "a certain kind of power in men, governments and peoples must do certain things or be broken."

The Case for African Freedom and *Britain and West Africa* are likewise founded on the idea of freedom set forth in *Power in Men*, but here there is a special application to a part of the world which Cary knows well, and to a vexed political situation of which he was for many years a part. He does not sentimentally suppose that the Africans were, in a state of nature, free. They were on the contrary enslaved by ignorance, by savagery, by inflexibility of the tribe. In any event, it is too late in the course of human history for mere withdrawal from Africa to take place. The clock cannot be turned back; the Africans will not allow it to be turned back. Having tasted liberty, they break eagerly from the constricting tribal organization which they now despise because it offers less freedom than what Europe has brought them. This is surely one of the themes of *Mister Johnson*, whose hero insistently and delightedly, but at last tragically, remakes the world in a larger and more generous image than he had thought possible in his childhood; his efforts to Europeanize his beloved Bamu by kissing her, marrying her from the Book of Common Prayer, and trying to persuade her to dress like an English lady—all these efforts illustrate his commitment to a larger and more satisfying view of the world.

Cary thus eschews the argument that the Europeanization of Africa has been a bad thing. He eschews equally the argument that it has been undertaken for disinterestedly benevolent motives. In *Britain and West Africa* he traces the colonization to a few individuals. "In history books," he says, "which must be full of dates and institutions, it is easy to lose sight of history itself which is made by men, all singular, all full of their private creeds and passions. We read of companies and governments, but the chief interest of West Africa lies in the men who made it; adventurers and poets of action; at their worst very close to pirates, at their best not far from monomaniacs, but always free and independent. For this reason they were extremely hard to manage by any kind of government."

THEME: THE POLITICS OF FREEDOM

The answer to Africa lies not in ignoring the actual situation but in recognizing it for what it is. *The Case for African Freedom* is a case; it is for allowing the Africans to learn how to use the freedom which is naturally and properly theirs. It is a plea for medical and economic assistance and for eventual withdrawal from Africa of such superimposed governments as that of which Cary himself was a part. It is a plea above all for education. Such counsel is bound to be maddening to extremists—to old-fashioned imperialists who resist the dismemberment of the Empire, as well as to African nationalists who abhor moderation and see in gradualism a rationale for eternal postponement. Nor does Cary see in this solution a method without friction, a smooth outcome. Real democracy is never smooth. "Freedom, power in the people, is a nuisance to rulers; it is insolent, enterprising, vulgar, inconstant, ungrateful," he says in *The Case for African Freedom*. "It produces in any state an everlasting confusion and turmoil. It has the manners of a yahoo and the vitality of a mad dog. But you cannot do without it because it is life itself and a dead State does not stink."

The course of human history is tragic; Cary's liberal creed takes too much account of history itself to embrace any idea of man's perfectibility. No closed system allows for man's real nature. "The typical Briton," as he tells the French in "L'influence britannique dans la révolution libérale", "prefers to collaborate with human nature in its known needs, [rather] than try to change it into something more amenable to reason and more obedient to the police. He feels in fact, even when he hardly recognizes his own convictions or their source, that man is essentially an individual, and that as an individual he has a unique claim to individual consideration." Cary is writing typically, but

39

is himself not a typical Briton. He goes further than the typical Briton. In "Roman à Thèse" he says, "How can a man, seeking his own way through the individual world of his individual experience, walk on the party line? He must be true to himself, or he will not give truth to others, the only truth he can give, his own experience." So besides rejecting the old liberalism, he rejects some at least of the new liberalism as well. "Men and women," he says in *The Case for African Freedom*, "are not units in an economic structure, they are living souls who are ready often to ignore even the primary needs of their bodies for some ideal satisfaction; glory or learning, religion or beauty." It is this fact, surely, which he dramatizes so convincingly in all his novels, not least in *The Horse's Mouth*. It is true that Gulley Jimson is defeated by the conservatism of the academy, that the bourgeois society of which he is inescapably a part rejects him, that he is eternally and fatally at odds with his environment. But it is equally true that Gulley would be as violently at war with any system, any formalization of the social structure—just as he is at war with form in his own art. It is impossible to imagine any Arts Council, however liberally constituted, that would satisfy him. Yet Cary, though entirely sympathetic with Gulley, does not himself embrace the anarchist's faith. "Anarchy," he writes in *Britain and West Africa*, "is the prime wretchedness of the poor and the weak."

But in a democracy which can steer the dangerous middle course between anarchy and any kind of fixed system, Cary sees the most substantial hope for man. He does not believe in 1984, because he does not believe that twentieth-century man, having been freed by education, by technological advance, by travel—having, that is, been given scope to exercise the freedom which is innate—Cary does not believe that twentieth-century man can acquiesce in what Orwell so grimly prophesies. "That is," he wrote me recently, "although there is no progress in happiness there is a process of development in history, a direction and, as far as I can see an irreversible direction, unless you can imagine all book education and technical knowledge being wiped out." Indeed, he sees an end to war "for lack of any state willing to undertake it." Thus he wrote in *Process of Real Freedom* in 1943, but thus he has written again and again since the war. In a broadcast in 1952, Cary looked not to the further disintegration of the world, not to a general collapse, but to a reintegration which would make possible the continued subsistence of civilization. Nevertheless, although Cary did not look back to any golden age, neither did he look forward to a time when man or society will be perfect, or even stable. "There will always be plenty of luck and bad luck in human affairs; there will always be suffering and disaster. If you have freedom, you have got to have evil in the world—you cannot get away from it."

3 Poetry

Cary's poems are of course intimately related in theme to the political writings, but the poetic themes are an expression of interests even more central to his view of man. Cary is not, I think, a great poet, and it is a comforting thought that *Verse*, which was published in Edinburgh in 1908 under the name of Arthur Cary, is almost unobtainable. Not even the British Museum possesses a copy of this work, which Cary in later life looked back on with distaste. "As far as I can remember," he wrote me (he could not be persuaded to reread these poems), "they were real trash; really very bad indeed for a boy of my age. But in Edinburgh I was moving in a peculiar atmosphere of sentimentalism, a kind of hangover of the greenery-yallery period or even earlier, late Rossetti." The poems are at best conventional. There is a sonnet on ambition, "that traitress, gaudy dressed"; there is another sonnet on nature—"I'll drink the mountain wind for purer wine"; there is another on withdrawal from the world. There is a song in mixed metre in celebration of a storm. There are half a dozen lines on suicide; there is a sportive triolet on melancholy. And there are 128 lines of rhymed tetrameter lamenting the fact that knowledge has destroyed the pleasures of innocence:

> *Dumb suspicion ruleth where*
> *Gentle mistress debonair*
> *Sang and told jolif and gay.*

And the Caroline verses which Middleton Murry used to see Cary writing on the floor when they were both living in Holywell—some at least of these survive in manuscript, where, I think, they had better remain. But *Marching Soldier* (1945) and *The Drunken Sailor* (1946) are a different matter, and they both deserve some attention here.

Marching Soldier is the shorter, the less ambitious, and the more successful of the two. The theme is war. The question which it poses and grapples with throughout is this:

> *We are reasonable men, old soldiers to whom the war*
> *   has issued*
> *Plenty of time to think, and to think again.*
> *Only tell us, if you know, who gives us the first orders?*
> *What truly makes the wheels go round?*

THEME: THE POLITICS OF FREEDOM

For the moment, in a dream, the narrator seems to have grasped the answer to his question; but when he awakens, the answer has eluded him. Later, in a conversation between the soldiers and some prisoners, the prisoners answer the question as follows:

> *Because of a man, a preacher.*
> *Because of a mouth that cried to us names,*
> *And the names walked among us like kings.*
> *At the sound of their feet*
> *Old leper poverty fell from our necks, cold idiot fear*
> *crept from our beds.*
> *The clouds rose from the sky, the oceans were drawn*
> *together in a cow-pool,*
> *The nations were a cabbage field, calling for our seed,*
> *The birds sang in our cellars, a loving wife took us*
> *by the hand*
> *To bring us to our field, our cow-pool, our little farm;*
> *With six pigs, six cows, and roses round the gate.*
> *And the wife was truth eternal, the roses were beauty*
> *that never withers,*
> *The field was peace everlasting.*
> *Because of a word, comrades, we went to war . . .*

This answer to the question asked at the beginning of the poem suggests Cary's preoccupation with the power of the word for good and evil. In the Carfax preface to *A Fearful Joy* he speaks of "the power of the spell-binder in history; the work of those 'artists' who, in preaching, creating, move the crowd; those who take their part among all artists in renewing life and the passion of life to peoples always growing bored or stale in their own achievement." He dilates on this subject in the political trilogy, and also in the novel on which he was working at the time of his death.

The Drunken Sailor is an allegory. The poem is written as though by a Blake heavily influenced by a Coleridge, a Yeats and an Eliot. The metre is rough and irregular. The sailor sings his celebration of the storm and of seamanship; he sings in praise of freedom:

> *Holy Father, Holy he be*
> *Who nailed us living to this tree*
> *Of our responsibility,*
> *Who damned our folly to be free*
> *On watch for all eternity*
> *Through boundless storm, nor ever see*
> *Peace but only victory*
> *Withering in its own hot breath,*
> *No rest but war's that sleeps on death*
> *And loves its mattress . . .*

The whole poem, and I think the whole of Cary's thinking, turns upon this tragic paradox: it is the glory and the tragedy of man that, possessed of the free imagination, he seeks fulfilment, which, however, is destroyed by the very act of fulfilment. Freedom and authority are ever at war, and if freedom wins in the contest, there is not "peace but only victory."

The Drunken Sailor expatiates somewhat complicatedly on this theme. There are marginal glosses, there is a narrator; the Dead speak, and the Fugitives speak also. "The privateer of imagination," one of the glosses reveals, "is challenged by the battleship of authority." And in the contest which follows, the free imagination triumphs by escaping authority. "But," says the gloss, "men of imagination feel no triumph, since by imagination they can grasp their fate, which is never to have repose. . . ." And finally, at the end of the poem, the gloss tells us that "imagination by its very nature must find in all completion a gaol, in all conclusion a grave." *The Drunken Sailor* is not, I think, a successful poem. It is too long, too freighted with devices, too insistently explicit: and though some of the description is wonderfully and characteristically just, fresh and affecting, the poetry as a whole—but particularly the rhyme—is forced. Cary is no Blake. On the other hand, the poem on account of its very explicitness is important in its setting forth of Cary's own artistic creed. For instance, in *The Horse's Mouth* Gulley Jimson's Sara-in-the-Bath phase is only a phase in his life; he goes beyond it and is constitutionally unable, even when offered the blandishments of money and recognition, to return to that stage. When he paints Sara, he finds in that completion a gaol, and seeking always to find further possibility of expressing his free imagination he moves from what he calls a lyric to an epic phase. He, like Cary himself, eternally seeks new forms through which he can express himself.

4 *Short Stories*

The short stories are equally useful to illustrate in briefer form and in simpler focus the themes of the novels, and they are interesting and important in their own right as well. They can best be considered in three groups: stories of Africa, stories of childhood, and stories of old age. Although such classification is not perfectly satisfactory, it has the utility of suggesting the main areas of Cary's work in this genre. Of the stories in each area I shall discuss only a few samples, and these only of the published work.

Of the African short stories, I have already alluded to one of the most important, "Bush River." Among the

others, "Umaru" stands out especially both for its qualities in itself and for its dramatization, against the exotic
background, of a major Cary theme. "Umaru," like "Bush
River," is a story of Nigeria in the First World War. It
turns on the relationship of young Captain Corner and his
aged sergeant, a Hausa named Umaru. On a stormy night
lying beneath the sky the two men talk, but not much; and
they only glancingly manage to communicate the idea to
each other, bridging the gaps of age, language and culture,
of man's loneliness in the immensity of the universe.
Communication is possible at bare human touch and at the
words, uttered by old Umaru, 'God prolong us.' And this
is a solace, a source of "a serene enjoyment." Elsewhere—
in his essay called "Roman à Thèse"—Cary has treated
this subject descriptively. "Wittgenstein," he remarks
"has said, that everyone has his own world. I should rather
say that men are together in feeling, in sympathy, but
alone in mind." And it is in this context that the theme of
isolation, which is of course an outstanding feature of
twentieth-century literature, must be always considered in
Cary's work. In *Mister Johnson* Celia Rudbeck and
Johnson's wife Bamu fail to communicate; the fact that they
speak different languages is but one aspect of this failure,
which arises really from the collision between very
different worlds. There is the terrible loneliness of Charley
Brown in *Charley is My Darling*, a loneliness assuaged
from time to time by his disastrous love affair with a
significantly deaf farm girl. For—and Cary says it, shows
it, again and again—man is isolated just because he is free.

This theme is thus found in the short stories of childhood
as well. "A Special Occasion," for instance, closely parallels
"Umaru." The occasion is special because Jenny, a little
girl in a party frock, is allowed to play with Tommy in his

nursery. When the children meet, ordinary language does not enable them to communicate directly. They are just beginning to establish a relationship obliquely—he is making an engine go round his track as fast as possible, she is reading his book—when the nurse comes into the room and berates Tommy for not playing with the girl. Though he denies misbehaviour, the nurse takes Jenny away. But soon the little girl returns, and it is this act— though neither of them realizes it consciously, and though the fact is not stated directly—that re-establishes the lines of communication between them. At last the girl gives "an enormous sigh of relief, of happiness." So the establishment of sympathy makes this a special occasion in another way.

But it is discovery altogether that is the major concern of the stories of childhood. In "Romance," two girls have a tug-of-war with a tiny baby, until the mother of one of the girls rescues the baby and drives the girls away. But one of them returns and smacks the baby. It is a gesture at once imitative of mature behaviour and expressive of her own inability to make the imitation altogether success-ful. The girl is trying to discover the limits and possibilities of a world whose map she has not yet charted. Imitation of gesture as a route to discovery is also the theme of "Carmagnole," an extremely short story whose setting is a children's party. A baby, younger than the rest of the children, toddles into the drawing room and wets the pink carpet. The children are horror-struck, silent—until a parlour-maid comes into the room, observes the puddle, and breaks into helpless giggles. Now the children know how to deal with this situation; their response imitates the parlour-maid's; they dance and jump and somersault for joy. And in "A Glory of the Moon"—"The Children," it begins, "were playing funerals"—a child becomes aware, no doubt for the first time, of the fact of death. A little girl lies in an orange box, pretending to be a corpse, while a boy pretending to be a parson intones words half-remembered from church. But the little girl suddenly sobs, and when the boy asks her what is wrong, she replies,'I don't know.'

"Spring Song" deals with language; it is a nonsense piece, but like all nonsense it obeys rules strictly logical. Two children, Margaret and Tom, are taken for a walk by their bespectacled elder sister, in the course of which Margaret invents a story, and thus a world, with nonsense words that bear a relation to the world she already knows: she is in the process of creating her own world by extending the boundaries she is already aware of. Part of her delight as she invents this new universe of new words (a universe of the akkerpeetie man made of fish bones who possesses a toople with black whiskers, the toople being not a dog but a singum because 'it came from Baffrica where all the dogs are scats') is the delight of knowing that words are capable of such extension. Nor is Margaret thwarted even when her sister reproaches her for this nonsense, for the young girl has won the applause of her brother, as well as the satisfaction of her own delight. When, at the end of the story, Gladys scolds Margaret, Margaret scolds her doll—but in nonsense: 'Lie down Vera, or I'll give you such a smack on your poly.'

Between extreme youth and extreme age there is, as several of Cary's stories show, a special sympathy: discovery and recovery go hand in hand. The best of these, "Success Story," records an old man's triumph over his frail body, and his triumph of sympathetic communication with a small boy. The old man, wearing ancient clothes,

comes unsteadily into a park and plants himself on a bench.
When a three-year-old boy comes along, sympathy is
established between them as the old man urges on the
boy's imaginary horse. The boy is delighted, and so is the
old man. Then the boy jumps on to the bench and from
there to the old man's knees. The old man is as terrorized
as the boy is enchanted—and the child has no perception
of the suffering which he is causing. But at last the boy,
having been dragged away by his sister, leaves the old
man "broken in, ravaged like a pie after a birthday party."
The child immediately forgets the old man, who after some
moments, makes an effort to rise from the bench. "At last
he stood upright. He raised his chin, a trembling hand
went up to set the hat straight. For a moment he stood.
Then all at once he lifted his stick about two inches and
struck its iron ferule hard upon the gravel. He had done it
again."

5 *Unpublished Work*

The amount of Cary's unpublished work is vast. There are
two plays, the manuscripts of which survive; there are
many unpublished short stories and essays; and literally
millions of words of novels and fragments of novels. Some
of these I have, unfortunately, been unable to find. Cary
told me that the first novel he wrote, about 1912, was
about students in Paris. I cannot find the manuscript. Nor
can I find his second novel, *William*, which he wrote
toward the end of his African service—that is, between the
years 1918 and 1920. He recalled having sent it to A. P.
Watt, but that distinguished agent was evidently unable
to place it for him. There is another novel also of this
period, a work called *Markby*, which is evidently no longer

extant. Cary could remember about it only the fact that it was probably written after *William*.

And in Cary's house were many tantalizing boxes of fragments which I cannot discuss here. Let me simply mention some of them. *To Sleep in Ulro*, also called *Hamper*, is a fragment about a famous fashion designer who commits suicide. Cary said he began it as a "bit" of *A Fearful Joy*, and undertook to dramatize the idea of fashion as "a pure aesthetic object." There are also large chunks of a projected trilogy to be called *The Captive and the Free* (a title which he liked, for he used it, as I have said, for his last novel); this trilogy, which was abandoned, concerns itself with the economic background of the 'twenties and 'thirties. There is *The Homely Nurse*, a fantasy on eugenics. There is *The Come Back* (about 1948), the story of an old actor named Fuljam who has gone down in the world but who is rediscovered by a B.B.C. producer looking for "originals." Besides this fragment there are in manuscript works called *Tottenham* (Cary remembered this as a "pathetic story about a little boy who was teased at school"); *The Foleys*, *Todd* and other works which I am now going to discuss in greater detail, as representative both of Cary's novelistic preoccupations and of what proved less tractable to his talent than what has already been published. These are *Cock Jarvis*, *Arabella*, which is complete, *Marta* and *The Heiress*.

The longest unfinished novel is *Cock Jarvis*, the length of which Cary estimated to be half a million words. Jarvis, whom Cary described in a 1956 broadcast to be "a Conrad character in a Kipling rôle," appears in *Castle Corner* and is alluded to in *The African Witch*. "He had," Cary says, "a high sense of honour and duty like Kipling's soldiers but he was also essentially liberal in sympathy." This

THEME: THE POLITICS OF FREEDOM

Jarvis, of *Cock Jarvis*, is a more complex character than the young man depicted in *Castle Corner*, and Cary could not, in earlier years, handle him. "My problem," he said in the broadcast, "was to show that though Jarvis was right in principle he was wrong in fact because the Empire couldn't last—it was up against powers that would certainly destroy it and the problem was therefore to dissolve or transform it in such a way that it wouldn't be succeeded by a thousand years of barbarism, war and misery." But in the 1920s Cary had not yet discovered forms which could contain this intuition of the everlasting revolution; and he found, as even the early unpublished work shows, that he must not try to crowd the whole world on to a single canvas.

Arabella, however, is complete. This novel was written in the middle 1930s, and it represents, Cary said, an early effort to get away from the African setting. *Arabella* is a political fantasy—taking political, as it must always be taken in Cary's works, in its broadest sense. The novel is satiric, philosophical, prophetic. The target of the satire is governments, or rather any kind of governmental system which would dehumanize man. Nazis and Communists are interchangeable; there is in fact in this novel a kind of fore-shadowing of 1984. But whereas Orwell was writing, in this period, *The Road to Wigan Pier*, that movingy and uneasy apology for socialism, Cary was already set against any such systematization of human beings.

The principal figure in *Arabella* is Professor Willie Hoopey, the victim and the disciple of both Nazism and Communism. He is credulous, intelligent, learned; Cary told me that Hoopey was suggested to him by the character of Bertrand Russell. Hoopey's journey to Paris and a series of taxi accidents, to Germany and the Nazis, to Soviet Russia and a Sovietized Washington, is a progress from one inadequate philosophical position to another. Although from the beginning, as a Blake-quoting believer in man as an artist, he is anti-violent, and remains so in the face of violence, his journey is necessary before he can discover that behind systems, above man, beyond philosophy, is God.

Arabella is not a great novel, and it found no publisher. It is not as even in tone as the novels of Evelyn Waugh which were being published in that decade. There is, in *Arabella*, an incompatible marriage of action and comment about action. The pace is too hectic. There is too much incident. Yet there are some wonderfully fine moments, as when an international banker called Fearstunt Gorgon goes to Russia disguised as a bear, and when Professor Hoopey delivers a speech in Russia which his interpreter, anxious that Hoopey should please the audience, translates in reverse. The book as a whole gives valuable evidence of the sort of experiment which Cary undertook before he found a technique adequate to the expression of his political intuition.

Marta is a fragmentary novel written in the 1930s. The book begins in Occam Street, in the middle of a London slum, where an ancient bag of bones (closely resembling the old Sara Monday, as she is depicted in *The Horse's Mouth*) falls brokenly and heavily to the pavement. When the police are sent for and she is searched, she is discovered to be Lady Portlock, whom the elderly editor of the *Evening Mail* remembers to have been Marta Armfeld—'She was one of the Marlborough House circle—one of the Prince of Wales beauties. One of the best of them.'

The second chapter takes the reader back to Marta's childhood. She is a girl "with a round face, very pale straight hair, a bulging forehead and thick short legs," a self-sufficient girl whom nothing will spoil. When she goes to school she is good tempered, high spirited and popular. When at last she is presented—"at the first court of 1877"—she begins to enjoy the life of a debutante. She is extremely busy and popular, but she looks toward "something better, something more permanent and above all more satisfying." She meets the Prince of Wales, and because he notices her she becomes celebrated. She is invited everywhere. At last she meets Felix Portlock, a young man of liberal and evangelical sympathies—surely an early version of Chester Nimmo, or even of Bonser. And, although she is sought after by a soldier named Dick Hamlin (a version of Jim Latter), she marries Portlock.

Ten years later Hamlin comes into her life again. "To talk with Dick was to talk with Dick, a true and real person; to talk with Felix was to deal with a complicated mass of purposes, schemes, aspirations, moralities; a political party held together by a common self-interest. . . . You do not love a political party, even with the highest ideals. You love a person and the centre of a person is truth." So rationalizes Marta in exactly the same way that Nina Latter rationalizes about the two men in her life; and, like Nina, she has an affair with the soldier.

This fragment, however, is not the political trilogy in miniature. For Marta has not become, nor does she become, a prisoner of grace to her husband. He has not Chester's complexity or his force. Nor does he become corrupt. Dick Hamlin is also simpler, and Marta is soon bored with him; for, except for his physical passion, he is a dull man. She terminates her affair with him, and afterwards "she had changed. She was changed into a woman who could find no happiness in love or anything else; who was never at peace; who was compelled to pass her whole life doing things that she detested in order to escape from still more detestable things; from failure, humiliation, boredom." And at this point, though there are also a couple of chapters about her son at school, the story of Marta Portlock breaks off.

Of *The Heiress*, which exists in a number of fragments and under a variety of titles, Cary also spoke in his 1956 broadcast on his unfinished work. *The Heiress* is the story of a young girl at a dance who is not danced with until the handsomest young man there asks her. Then she has an enchanting evening. "But," Cary said, "the young man's reason is not that he has suddenly seen the charms of a rather plain and very badly dressed girl, but that he has been told she is an heiress. And afterwards she finds this out." Years later, Cary says, this idea became the basis for *A Fearful Joy*. But the story of the girl at the dance had to be removed. "I saw that the book needed a solider, more historical first chapter. . . ."

In view of the finished achievement of *A Fearful Joy*, it is worth looking at some of the rejected pieces of this novel before it became a novel. One early version is called *Juno*, a girl described in a note on the manuscript as "an heiress and under trustees . . . who don't bother and leave her to the aunt—the fashionable woman. She is sold and robbed and this suits her." In the fragmentary manuscript Juno is described as a young Amazon. She is the despair of her family because she seems stupid and queer. In another version, called *Facts of Life*, there is Toner, a smuggler and half-crook "in command of his own destiny . . . afraid of nothing and nobody." He meets Betty Wendt, a young girl who is an heiress, pretty and wilful. Another beginning is as follows: "When Betty Wendt the ice cream heiress got her fourth divorce, everybody said either 'the worthless creature' or 'poor little rich girl','" and then the narrator begins to describe her meeting with Phil Toner. In still another beginning she is divorced and "now an amateur ready to sleep with any personable man, and, indeed, preferring the chance stranger." None of these beginnings worked; none of them is as satisfactory as the opening of *A Fearful Joy*. But all demonstrate the tireless energy, the insistent inventiveness, with which Cary attacked his subjects.

Among the unpublished works there are, as I have said, two plays. Written in the 1930s and never produced, they deserve discussion here not so much for their dramatic quality as for their preoccupation with what is at the heart of all Cary's work: a religious intuition. Both plays are set in Africa, each contains a prophetic figure, and in each play this figure is a well-educated African.

The first play, *Happy Valley*, centres around a film, a rather bad and vulgar extravaganza, which is being made in Africa. The principals in this enterprise are quarrelsome, superficial, emptily energetic. The film directors plan, for their *pièce de résistance*, to instal a swimming pool in a temple. From the pool will emerge the heroine, who will there converse with the priest. Such is the tone of the directors' minds. The author of the scenario acquiesces in this specious nonsense and—in real life—plans an adulterous elopement with one of the actresses, who is married to one of the directors—while the author's wife, an invalid, establishes a sympathetic relationship with the District Commissioner, a plain and simple and suspicious young man. Every one of the English characters of *Happy Valley* lacks a will to live, or anything to live by. Into their midst comes Mponyi, perhaps too obviously prophetic; he is well educated, black, a so-called faith healer. In a scene with the English film-makers he lays bare the shallowness of their lives and challenges them to live more deeply, by which he means more honestly self-appraisingly.

His "cure" of the author's wife is typical. He simply sets forth what he conceives to be the truth about life, which is "that life is hard and dangerous; that he who seeks his own happiness, does not find it; that he who is weak, must suffer; that he who demands love, will be disappointed; that he who is greedy, will not be fed; that he who seeks peace, will find strife; that truth is only for the brave; that joy is only to him who does not fear to be alone; that life is only for the one who is not afraid to die." This is the centre of the play, which is in fact a comedy; for all the film-makers, having responded to Mponyi, are at last restored to a health which depends not upon a shallow optimism or a deliberate myopia, but upon a faith in the certainty of good as well as in the inevitability of evil.

The King is Dead, Long Live the King is even more direct. Here is a conventional situation, white civil servants in conflict with Africans. The colonials want peace, things as they are; the Africans wish to elevate to chieftainship Isa Dan Siriki, a young man who has been educated in England and who has travelled in Europe. He belongs to the local royal house, but he is not the only candidate for the throne. The fact that he has many supporters makes the acting governor and others regard him with suspicion; he is thought to be a troublemaker. In fact, he is enlightened and civilized. He wants to start schools. He wishes to enable the native civilization to break out of its narrow tribal circle. He wants to teach the spirit of God. But he is personally unambitious; he does not want to become chief. Nevertheless, some of the people so proclaim him. His speech of acceptance deals with the spirit of God, and it is more explosive than he intends. He is, after a brief period in hiding, dragged off to prison, where he is tortured and at last put to death. But his tragedy, like all real tragedy, irradiates its surroundings; death destroys Isa Dan Siriki, but the idea of death, his death, saves the others.

Like his tireless technical experiment and like the facts of his career, Joyce Cary's minor works demonstrate altogether a life-long commitment to the writer's craft. They show a relentless energy. They bear witness to the success and the failure which had to precede or accompany the distinction of the best of his novels. For it is as a novelist that Cary's achievement has been brilliant, original, relevant. It is as a novelist that Cary's ambition, to draw a map of the landscape of existence, is realized. This landscape all can recognize, because it is a picture of ourselves.

6 *Novels of Africa*

The African novels—*Aissa Saved, An American Visitor, The African Witch* and *Mister Johnson*—are all early and they all provide a setting in which Cary can depict in clear and simple contrasts his theme of man's freedom and the world he creates in order to give it scope. None of these novels is colonial, even in the sense that *A Passage to India* is colonial. Their interest is not in explaining Africa to England, not in making a plea for this or that course of action vis-à-vis Nigeria; the interest is in the drama played against a backdrop which by its very brilliance lays bare human motivation. As Cary says in "My First Novel," there is in Africa, "confusion, conflict, the destruction of old values before the new are established. But this is the perpetual situation of the whole world—it always has been." That is, the interest in an exotic setting is of the same order as Conrad's; it is metaphysical: Cary does in fact acknowledge Conrad as one of his masters.

Aissa Saved begins with a description which invites comparison with the opening of *A Passage to India*. Each describes a site upon a river, but Forster's opening is sophisticated ("the Ganges happens not to be holy here"), Cary's is plain. Forster sees India as a traveller, as a sympathetic observer from Bloomsbury; Cary sees Africa from within. But Cary's motive is different, too. Forster writes of a conflict of cultures as exemplifying, and also symbolizing, the fundamental isolation of human beings. Speculation fails. The religious experience is an empty echo in a cave. But *Aissa Saved*, springing from a religious perception, exhibits the relationship of men and their faiths. More particularly Cary's book, as he says in "My First Novel", "deals with individual religion, that is to say, the beliefs or unconscious assumptions which actually govern conduct. These assumptions are different in every person. That is to say, everyone has his own faith. Of course each great religion does draw large numbers of people together in general rules of conduct, and general statements of belief. But each person makes a particular application of the rules and mixes them up with a lot of other ideas and rules drawn from all kinds of sources. This is a fundamental situation due to the nature of things; the fact, for instance, that each individual has to think for himself, and that no religion can cover the infinite variety of problems thrown up to quite ordinary people, living quite ordinary lives."

Aissa, a beautiful half-breed, is a woman of spirit: a savage partly liberated from savagery; upon her alternations between Christianity as she understands it and the native religion on which she has been raised the movement of the book depends. Christianity, primitively understood, and ju-ju, which can be understood in no other way, are both inadequate; but *Aissa Saved* is not meant to condemn organized religion, it is an exploration of the expression of the religious instinct. That Aissa both succeeds and fails, that her success and failure are equally fragile, that no final resolution is possible until death itself—these are the glorious and the fatal outcomes of freedom.

An American Visitor also treats this theme. Marie Hasluck, the American visitor to Nigeria, is a natural anarchist; with a faith, therefore, that moral choices can be made correctly only in an atmosphere free of restraints of any kind. She has a belief in man's innate goodness, in his ability to make his own laws *ad hoc*. She distrusts traditional authority, represented here in the person of the District Officer Bewsher, as not only constricting and limiting but also stultifying and destructive. It is a tragic dilemma, one which cannot be solved by mediation.

Freedom's direction is, of course, toward anarchy, and Marie Hasluck's brand of romanticism is widely supposed to be a feature of the American temperament. At least her type very often appears in novels, one of the latest examples being that of the American in Graham Greene's *The Quiet American*. Not that a comparison between the two books can be pressed. Greene's American becomes, by the breadth of his naïveté, villainous; Cary's American is more sympathetically regarded. For Cary, though he like Greene can rail against those who will not give law its due, nevertheless recognizes "the faith which lies behind anarchism" as necessary and desirable. "If," he says in the Carfax preface to *An American Visitor*, "none had ever rebelled against the law in the name of freedom, we should still be living in the stone-age under the tyranny of some ju-ju priest-king or tribal Politburo."

If *An American Visitor* is an uneven and finally unsatisfactory novel, the reason is that Marie Hasluck is an idea rather than a human being. When he wrote this book Cary had yet to see America for the first time; and the characterization of the heroine suffers from second-handedness. To compare Marie to any of the Africans or to any of the English characters in this novel is to acknowledge her thinness. Furthermore, in the last quarter of the novel she gives first place to Gore the official and Cottee the prospector, whose somewhat summary ruminations serve all too patently as vehicles for Cary's theme. To dramatize rather than narrate, to embody rather than preach, to direct rather than describe—these require, besides great technical skill, knowledge at first hand. From such knowledge comes *The African Witch*.

The truth about the human situation as Cary dramatizes it in *The African Witch* is, as always, complex. The conflicts between human beings cannot be resolved so long as men remain men, energetically asserting the freedom which is the power that makes men human in that it gives them choice. And, tempting as it is to read *The African Witch* as a colonial novel, it must be considered in the wider context which is always Cary's first interest: the context of men, rather than Africans or Englishmen or Africans versus Englishmen. Considered in this light, the witch Elizabeth Aladai assumes an importance which might otherwise be forgotten. She is the spellbinder who as a human type is to be found not only in Nigeria but everywhere. Her power for good and evil depends in large part upon a rhetorical skill which Cary treats again, and much more fully, in the political trilogy in the person of Chester Nimmo.

Mister Johnson, the last and the simplest of the African novels, is certainly the best. Johnson himself, the less than half-educated clerk whom Cary describes in the Carfax preface as a "poet who creates for himself a glorious destiny," is a fascinating creation, one of the most fully realized characters in the entire canon. And in this book Cary finds a structure—a plain story of love and friendship —and a style—the present tense—perfectly adapted to his needs. In *Mister Johnson* Cary is able to avoid the manipulative plotting which lames the ending of *Aissa Saved*; he is able to eschew the proliferation of characters which divide the interest of the other three novels of Africa; he is able to dramatize rather than relate. Having published four other novels, Cary in *Mister Johnson* hits his stride— and it is probably not irrelevant to record that he found this the easiest of all his books to write.

In the four novels of Africa Cary draws a map which performs the service of pointing the way to his other works. *Aissa Saved* displays, somewhat paradoxically but with perfect simplicity, the appetite for religious experience that can be thwarted but never gainsaid. In *An American Visitor* there is Cary's preoccupation with the impulse to anarchy that can be modified but never expunged. *The African Witch* reveals, very harshly but with entire objectivity, the power of spellbinding that can be tempered but never effaced. Mister Johnson himself is the embodiment of that power to create in spite of all impediments which is to find profounder realization in Gulley Jimson. This is not to suggest that these novels are worth reading simply because they prefigure Cary's later work, although they do accomplish this purpose. For the African novels, *Aissa Saved* and

61

Mister Johnson especially, command attention and respect because they exhibit a sense of the collision of cultures, a sense which does not subsist in isolation, because it is an aspect of the inevitable clashes between free men.

The African Witch, Cary writes in the Carfax preface, and what he says applies with equal force to the other African novels, is not meant as an attack on colonial policy or as a work on the colour bar. "My book," he says, "was meant to show certain men and their problems in the tragic background of a continent still little advanced from the Stone Age, and therefore exposed, like no other, to the impact of modern turmoil. An overcrowded raft manned by children who had never seen the sea would have a better chance in a typhoon." That is, Cary's interest is not in Africa as such. His interest is always in drawing a map of life that will do justice to the human situation as he observes it; and he sees the human situation as everywhere the same. Europe provides a patina of complexity; but beneath this lid of civilization is the fundamental human being whose capacity for being human is the same whatever the geography. And here lies the clue not only to his choice of Africa but also to his abandonment of that continent as his setting. For Africa, "just because it is dramatic, demands a certain kind of story, a certain violence and coarseness of detail, almost a fabulous treatment, to keep it in its place." But it is after all the complexity of European civilization to which Cary wishes to move. Having blazed his trail he can go, enlightened, back to England.

7 *Novels of Childhood*

To a second group of novels belong two works centring on childhood. These are *Charley is My Darling* and *A House*

THEME: THE POLITICS OF FREEDOM

of Children. In childhood as among the Nigerians Cary
finds his theme expressed clearly and very simply. The
difference between Mister Johnson, the young African
clerk, and Charley Brown, the delinquent evacuee, is hardly
more than that of pigmentation. The childlike African and
the childlike adolescent—they are almost of an age—are
in the throes of creation, seeking desperately and comically,
but finally disastrously, to shape worlds satisfying to themselves.

Charley is My Darling opens in the autumn of 1939 when
Charley Brown, a fifteen-year-old evacuee, arrives in the
West Country from London, and has to have his head
shaved because it is lousy. So the novel turns in the first
place on the radical dislocation of war. Charley as an
adolescent is trying to make the world out; he is discovering himself; the fact that he is an evacuee compounds but
does not alter the nature of his effort. Charley is also
delinquent. But, as Cary says in the Carfax preface, "it has
always seemed to me that every child is by nature a
delinquent, that the only difference between us as children
was the extent of our delinquency, whether we were found
out in it and how we were punished for it." *Charley is My
Darling,* therefore, goes beyond its immediate concern
with a matter that was in 1940 of great topical interest; it
becomes a novel of anguished late childhood in which geographical dislocation and actionable delinquency become
metaphorical extensions of the eternal attempt of im-
maturity to grow. And in *A House of Children* Cary takes
us back to his own early childhood in Ireland. This
explicitly autobiographical novel is the recollection of a
mature man who would re-view the world which he himself created. Violence, wonder and joy characterize both the
geography and the personal relations of this childhood.

63

Terror is not absent, and more than one parallel can be drawn between this book and Wordsworth's *Prelude*. But Cary's romanticism, such as it is, contains an astringency that prevents nostalgia from becoming remorseful. The direction is not inward, toward imprisonment; it is toward a world narrower indeed, but without any question more intense, than that of childhood. In *A House of Children*, writing as Evelyn Corner but also, I think, from his own heart, Cary says, "Grown-ups live and love, they suffer and enjoy far more intensely than children; but for the most part, on a narrower front. For the average man or woman of forty, however successful, has been so battered and crippled by various accidents that he has gradually been restricted to a small compass of enterprise. Above all, he is perplexed. He has found out numerous holes and inconsistencies in his plan of life and yet he has no time to begin the vast work of making a new one. . . . I think that is the reason for the special sadness of nearly all grown-up faces, certainly of all those which you respect; you read in their lines of repose, the sense that there is no time to begin again, to get things right. The greater a grown man's power of enjoyment, the stronger his faith, the deeper and more continuous his feeling of the waste of life, of happiness, of youth and love, of himself."

Charley is My Darling records, as it were from within, the painful isolation, the relentless necessity for exploration, the blind and urgent groping toward love, which constitute the inevitable shape of childhood. Built on a metaphorical structure of geographical dislocation, the novel moves through the shadows of the world's mysteriousness as they appear to Charley himself. *A House of Children*, since it has a different motive, has a different structure. This book, which Cary acknowledged to be autobiographical and which is set in Northern Ireland, is undertaken by Evelyn Corner, a man in middle years who will explore the past, his own childhood, in an effort to discover the route to himself. The fuchsia of the first page "took me," Cary writes in the Carfax preface, "not so much to memories as to the actual sensations of childhood, and I noticed, not for the first time, that these sensations are not always clearly related to the memories." The route is the method—from the sensation to the memory, from the senses to the imagination. So that, though chronological order is observed, the whole book as a recollection is held together not by progress in clock-time; the logic is that of feeling. As a book of rediscovery, as a summoning up of the past by a man forty years after the events have taken place, *A House of Children*, in explaining the child to the man, explains the man to himself.

Although they bear on every page the stamp of his special sympathy and his special quality, *Charley is My Darling* and *A House of Children* are not the most ambitious of Cary's novels. He wrote about children so well not only because he liked and respected them but because he understood both the completeness of their isolation and the urgency of their impulse to expression. Childhood's route to maturity is crooked. Clarity requires focus, focus requires narrowing of the vision: this indeed makes for the poignance as well as the consolation of the journey; and it is a journey which Cary, though he himself was perfectly clear about his idea of the world before he published his first novel, had to make novelistically before he could deal satisfactorily with the themes of his subsequent works; before, I should say, he had the novelistic experience that enabled him to embark on the great trilogies.

8 *Chronicles*

Cary's historical sense, his view of history as an eternal revolution in which destruction clears the way for new creation and new creation carries within it the seeds of decay—this sense, which haunted him as an artist and goes far to explain his restless technical experiment, finds expression in three novels whose interest is patently and centrally that of the chronicle. *Castle Corner* is the first of a projected trilogy which he abandoned after completing the first volume. It is a saga of a large Anglo-Irish family, a record of historical change, of the human forces behind this change, and of the effect which this change has upon the people involved. But, he felt, the canvas became too crowded, the characters unmanageable from a technical point of view. And he then turned with relief, as he says in the Carfax preface, to the simplicity of Africa again in *Mister Johnson*. The *Castle Corner* trilogy was abandoned for ever.

Castle Corner has no central focus. Of the ninety-three characters who appear in the book, none dominates the story, nor is there a sense that the generations of the Corner family impinge upon one another enough to provide continuity in this way. Also, the construction of the book is too often haphazard, as though Cary has more material than he can control; Castle Corner is saved from the fate of being wrecked by "a strange and lucky accident," which is that John Chass has a nosebleed and must return to the house to change his shirt: such puppeteering cannot be found in Cary's later work. Finally, Castle Corner itself does not constitute a symbol of sufficient strength to dominate the whole: Africa and England are geographically of nearly equal importance to Ireland in the novel. In short, there is such richness of characterization, story and setting in *Castle Corner* that the book fails on account of its very diffuseness to achieve the unity which is necessary in the construction of any novel.

Yet the book conveys the flavour of revolution, and not least in its characterization of the minor figures; these would be even more tantalizing had Cary not written more about them elsewhere, for they appear under other guises in the later novels. There is Mary Corner, John Chass's wife, a thoroughly Victorian woman whose collision with the liberated Helen Pynsant illustrates the revolution of the women in the period of which Cary is writing; there is Benskin, the South African millionaire, the new rich man who contrasts sharply with the declining Corners; there is Porfit, the earnest lay-preacher, a pacifist by conviction, who is surely an early version of Chester Nimmo of the political trilogy; there is finally a whole group of Irish characters from Manus Foy, the bitter Parnellite, to old Sukey Egan, the Castle Corner cook—all of whom, drawn with a few sure strokes, remain alive in the imagination. Nevertheless, the book because it is a failure in form is also a failure in theme. It remains a rough sketch.

The next chronicle is *The Moonlight*, between which and *Castle Corner* half a dozen novels intervene. *The Moonlight* is technically a much more experienced and much more successful work than the earlier chronicle. Here are three rather than a dozen main characters, and a conflict not between several but between two generations. There are an intransigently Victorian aunt, her "liberated" post-Victorian niece, and the mother of this girl, who mediates between the two generations. The excellence of this book lies in the sympathy which is evoked not for one generation against the other, but for both generations in conflict and in creation.

As a reply to Tolstoy's *Kreutzer Sonata*, *The Moonlight* turns inevitably on the subject of sexuality, especially female sexuality. Cary's aim is to show that beyond any system's power of imposition there exists a fundamental female nature which can be thwarted but never denied. Of Ella Venn, the central figure, a young man remarks, 'She's like a force of nature—they say mushrooms will lift a cathedral if they're put to it.' To this, Ella's daughter replies, 'I suppose they have to if they're going to live.' And almost resignedly the young man answers, 'The force of life might almost be measured in foot pounds.' Yet this is the point of emphasis, the specific example, in a novel whose wider interest is—as always in Cary's work—the perpetual revolution in belief, in taste, in morals, in faith. And while it is a measure of Cary's sympathy as well as of his understanding that this is not a book which extols "modern" values by pillorying the Victorian, neither does *The Moonlight* nostalgically try to rebuild the Victorian edifice. There is real question whether the young Amanda's neat, cold town life, whether Robin's modern perceptive bitterness, represent an advance on Rose's Victorian system of love by guilt. But as it is impossible not to sympathize with Rose—Cary as usual dares us to do so when, for instance, he shows her conveying her father's corpse to Florence Villa so that he can be said to have died at home rather than at his mistress's lodgings; and the reader must accept his dare—so is it impossible not to sympathize with Amanda, experimenting coolly if not always collectedly with her own nature, unable to be un-selfconscious, even in the act of love. But, like *Castle Corner*, *The Moonlight* fails on account of a division of interest. The book has no sustained "commanding centre": Ella, who is meant to fulfil this rôle, is too often pushed aside—particularly when the author finds it necessary, by means of much exposition, to introduce and characterize her sister's children. When Ella dies the book itself dies.

Finally, there is *A Fearful Joy*, the story of a woman living through a hundred revolutions, personal and historical, from the 1890s until after the Second World War. Her very life depends on acquiescing in what she often resists, the changes which must and do take place in the course of a long and lively life. Indeed there is within her the creative—the free—impulse, lighted and relighted by the imagination of Bonser, the man who becomes her husband; kindled and kindled again by her granddaughter and great-granddaughter. Tabitha is a superb creation, and it is not her fault that the book has an almost operatic lack of verisimilitude—it is the fault of the book's pace, not so much a too ambitious scope as an attempt to capture too many aspects of the revolution of the first half of the twentieth century. *A Fearful Joy* is like a film run too fast, a double-feature run through the projector at twice the ordinary speed.

In the Carfax preface, indeed, Cary records the difficulty he had with the book. "I am told," he says, "that the book is too packed, too fast moving, but I meant it to move quickly to give the sense of that driving change, of that world revolution which is so sharply present to our feelings from hour to hour. But the critics may be right. Since change is relative, I might have got my sense of movement less in succession of events than in contrast with some large permanent character; the 'family house,' the 'service tradition'." Perhaps, for the book which reads so excitingly leaves the reader at last curiously disappointed. And it is certain that Cary has written better elsewhere on this theme. But through and even by virtue of its very faults *A Fearful Joy* stands as an exemplification of Cary's attitude to the perpetual revolution. Cary is not concerned to show that the more the world changes the more it is the same; his interest is fixed, in *A Fearful Joy* as elsewhere, on the interaction between the forces of change and the forces of permanence.

A Fearful Joy is the last of Cary's attempts at the chronicle form, and though it is the most nearly successful of the three it cannot be called a success. Indeed, for all their richness and for all their brilliance, none of the chronicles succeeds in establishing a sustained atmosphere of felt life. *Castle Corner* fails just because of an over-richness—there are too many characters, there is too much happening, there is too much shift from place to place. *The Moonlight*'s central figure, Ella Venn, moves off the stage prematurely and leaves the book to limp unsatisfactorily to a conclusion. *A Fearful Joy*, though it is Tabitha's story from beginning to end and though she is a brilliant piece of characterization, attempts to capture too much of the history of more than half a century within the covers of a single book. The straightforward chronicle is not Cary's best method, because it is not Cary's style of thinking about the world: behind and beneath time is character, and it is the world as character that he can so brilliantly draw in the two trilogies which are his masterworks.

"A writer cannot drift on a stream," Cary says in "Roman à Thèse", "he is a man of action. He cannot even put words into the mouths of others without some grasp of the values implied by the speakers." This is true enough, and Cary took longer than most men to find a set of values which did justice to what he saw to be the actual

THEME: THE POLITICS OF FREEDOM

shape of the world. But it is one thing to have a vision, it is another to embody the vision. The art of writing a novel consists in deploying a set of characters convincingly, and this art Cary did not learn at once. But he knew that in the construction of a novel character comes first.

CHAPTER THREE

The World as Character

1 *The Three Characters*

IN the Carfax preface to *Herself Surprised* Cary asserts the primacy of character in the construction of the novel. Writing of the first trilogy altogether, he says, "The centre of the plan was character; the characters of my three leading persons in relation to, or in conflict with, other characters and the character of their times (and beyond that, of course, with 'final' character, I mean the shape of things and feelings which are 'given,' and which perhaps have to be so or nothing would exist at all)—the books had to be soaked in character." This is why, he says, his scheme did not come off as planned; he could not allow Sara to talk about art and history because "I found that she lost something of her quality and force; the essential Sara was diluted. . . . And in such a dilemma, whether to stick to my scheme, or to stick to character, the character as felt and known in the book, I stuck to my rule, which was character first."

But, although as a novelist Cary is a rich—indeed a prodigious—inventor, his range is severely limited. He is often compared to Dickens, but Dickens draws a whole gallery of individuals because for him idiosyncrasy is the defining aspect of man; Cary portrays again and again the same three people because for him it is the commonness of the human dilemma which is compelling. The man who must create, the man who would preserve, and the woman who as female resembles both the one and the other but also differs from either—these are the types to which Cary mainly confines himself because, for all their singularities, they constitute in Cary's world the defining limits of human possibility.

The first and most interesting type is the man who rejoices in freedom: the anarch, the artist, the man who destroys in order to create, the man who ignores all claims but his own. There is the megalomaniac District Officer of *An American Visitor* who resists all authority, who wishes to rule his district as absolutely as Kurtz in "Heart of Darkness," and who suffers the same fate. There is Louis Aladai, the Oxford-educated young claimant to the Rimi throne in *The African Witch*; he begins by trying to introduce European standards into his native land, and ends by ordering his sister to take away his European clothes. In *Castle Corner*, the free man is fragmented into several characters; and fragmentation is the fatal flaw of that novel. In the novels of childhood there are Charley Brown and Evelyn Corner, both swimming with the revolutionary tide because in revolution is self-discovery and creation. Finally, and culminatingly, there is the artist, whose very vocation it is to foment revolutions. The artist is sketched out in the Mr Lommax of *Charley is My Darling*, in the holiday tutor Pinto of *A House of Children* and in the superb rogue Dick Bonser of *A Fearful Joy*, the endlessly inventive entrepreneur whose imagination makes bright worlds. In Gulley Jimson and in Chester Nimmo, the one a politician in art and the other an artist in politics, Cary's characterization of man as everlasting artificer becomes fully and, I think, triumphantly realized.

Opposed to the revolutionary is the man attached to the past because there can be found certainty, continuity, civilization; opposed to the revolution because in creating it destroys, but condemned, like Tom Wilcher, to be a pilgrim. If the artist most truly represents the first of Cary's types, the lawyer and the soldier, those guardians of the heritage, most adequately represent the second. Gore in *An American Visitor*—he is, I am sure, an early version of Tom Wilcher—tries endlessly to reconcile the claims of sound government with the aims of Monkey Bewsher, or rather he tries to reconcile Bewsher to obeying the rules. Cock Jarvis, the patriotic young soldier of *Castle Corner*, is the younger brother of the fanatical Jim Latter; the Latter of *Not Honour More* is simply young Cock Jarvis become middle-aged, disillusioned and desperate. Bill Wilcher the soldier and Thomas Wilcher the lawyer of *To be a Pilgrim* represent two facets of the conservative mind, the one accepting the world and doing his duty, the other entrapped by the past and sentenced to the dutiful life.

I have said that Cary does not take sides. He presents his people disinterestedly. This is not, of course, because he is indifferent to the outcome but because his sympathies are so broad that he can feel the poignance of Tom Wilcher's defeat as keenly as he can Gulley Jimson's. But having been so objective in his presentation Cary does at last choose between them. He chooses the creative man. This is why Gulley's defeat is a triumph, and Wilcher's pathetic; this is why Chester Nimmo's defeat, for all that Cary makes us despise him, is a tragedy, and Jim Latter's fate sordid.

Mediating between these opposites is the female. Cary draws heavily on Blake for his idea of womanhood. The feminine principle is the completing and at the same time the destructive principle. "She nails him down upon a rock," Blake says in "The Mental Traveller," and "Catches his shrieks in cups of gold." It is the caught shrieks in the anguish of fulfilment which are the expressed creation of

74

man. Cary's women perform the creative rites of temptation and seduction; having done so, they build nests and
try, as Gulley says of Sara Monday, to domesticate their
men. Aissa, the heroine of Cary's first novel, is so fully
engaged in the war between Christianity and paganism
that she has little time for domestic pursuits, but she understands Christianity only in exclusively female terms: her
first communion means so much to her because she supposes that Jesus is having sexual intercourse with her; and
when there comes a test of strength between the Christian
doctrine to which she adheres fanatically and the female
nature which calls her back to her lover Gajere, she does
not hesitate to rejoin Gajere. Marie Hasluck of *An
American Visitor* is to a certain extent de-sexed by her
intellectual emancipation, but she succumbs at last to her
female nature. She becomes the mistress, then the wife and
finally the widow of Bewsher, from whom she learns that
what she thought about life was simply thought about in-
experience. Elizabeth Aladai, the African witch herself, is
no doubt the most formidable of all Cary's women. She is
so strong that she domesticates even her own brother, the
young man with the English education, and she destroys
one male after another in her insatiable greed for domesti-
cation of the male to her female needs. In *Castle Corner* all
the women know and cherish their function as mistress,
wife and mother, the Corner women no less than the Irish
peasants and the African woman who becomes the sometime wife of Felix Corner. In the novels of childhood three
girls stand out especially—the deaf and stupid Lizzie
Galor, who knows simply by instinct that to love and
succour Charley Brown is her rôle in life; and, in *A House
of Children*, Frances and Delia, the one an easy cherishing
mother and wife from her first maturity, the other, more

vital, sparked by the imagination of Pinto with whom she elopes. And are not the women of Cary's later novels all of a piece? Sara Monday, the eternal Eve, the perpetual nest builder, the triumphant mother: the woman whose symbol and home is the kitchen; Ella Venn, of a different class, whose affirmation of sexuality is an affirmation of her female nature, even in an age which stresses duty at the expense of nature; Tabitha Baskett, possessed of greater intelligence than either Sara or Ella, but condemned like them both to make very much the same pilgrimage, though over different ground and at a faster pace; and finally Nina, the brightest and most complicated of them all, imprisoned by grace to a man whom she detests, imprisoned equally by a life-long love to a man whom she cannot respect.

Cary is one of the giants among twentieth-century novelists, but he did not become so until he invented the novel of the triple vision; nor, having made this discovery, was he at his best when he abandoned it—as he did in *The Moonlight* and *A Fearful Joy*. He began, like many other artists, conventionally; and, despite *Mister Johnson* and *A House of Children*, he did not hit his best stride until the interconnected *Herself Surprised*, *To be a Pilgrim* and *The Horse's Mouth*. But seven novels precede this first trilogy. For what Cary discovered was that his genius for impersonation exactly meshed with the idea which animates but does not always bring fully alive his earlier works. Impersonation, as Felix Krull discovered, has its drawbacks as well as its advantages. So when Cary wrote *The Horse's Mouth* he was besieged with letters written from the supposition that Gulley Jimson and his creator were the same; *Not Honour More* was not translated into German until Cary wrote a preface explaining that he was not Jim Latter; and a girl who came to Cary's house to be a housekeeper almost changed her mind when, by way of preparing herself for her job, she read *To be a Pilgrim*. The scheme of this chapter, therefore, aims at showing how Cary in his characterization worked toward what became the inevitable style of the two trilogies. "What I'm after," Cary said in a broadcast in 1955, "[is] to show character in depth and how it works in a world which is itself a character."

2 *The Free Man*

By the end of the 1920s Cary had worked out, very largely by himself, the idea of the world which is at the centre of all his novels. But, as his early work shows, he could not embody that idea fully because he could not make the novelistic form yield the kind of result which he sought. He had seen and understood but he could not create the characters who would embody, nor could he control the structure which could contain, his vision. Indeed, I think it is fair to say that the first four of his novels are all, as novels, unsuccessful experiments. In his fifth, *Mister Johnson*, he produced a small but nonetheless considerable masterpiece. However, it would be wrong to assert that thenceforward Cary worked with the cool certainty of having found adequate form for his intuition. He never stopped struggling and he never stopped failing: the trilogies are separated by a brace of novels, *The Moonlight* and *A Fearful Joy*, which simply cannot compare to the best of his works; and the forms of the two trilogies themselves, though they have the inevitability of great art, were painfully and uncertainly arrived at before they were seized upon.

Aissa Saved is dominated by Aissa, and I intend to

consider her in due course, but there appears in that work no one man who can represent what always needs to be represented in a Cary novel—the creator, the artist, the revolutionary: the free man, making a free world for himself. But there are fragments of this man in the missioner Carr, who more than half stupidly but also kindly will impose a picture-book Christianity upon the Africans; in the District Officer Bradgate who plunges himself into the enterprise of building a bridge; and, above all, in the young African boy Ali who is en route by way of education to freedom. In fact, Ali was the germ of *Aissa Saved*. In the Carfax preface Cary records having known such a boy. He walked a hundred and thirty miles without sleeping, to help Cary make a map. This journey, which nearly killed the boy, was striking as "the effect of education on this rather shy and not very clever boy. . . . I was anxious to contrast Ali's standards and ideas with those above him. This, of course, involved questions of local ethics, local religion, the whole conflict of those ideas in a primitive community; and also the impact of new ideas from outside." But, in the course of writing the book, "Aissa gradually became the heroine because she was more central to a deeper interest, that of religion." Actually, I think Cary did not know how to handle Ali, who does not appear at all until nearly half-way through the book, and whose rôle is very small.

Ali, who is sixteen, is the son of the local Waziri—that is, the prime minister—and he has been to the government school. He explains to his fellow-countrymen who are anxious to make a sacrifice to the goddess of mountains and fertility, and who wish to put Aissa to death because they think she is a witch, that "witches had no power over rain which fell from the clouds when they were made cold, and besides all knew very well that it was a wrong thing to

condemn anybody without a proper trial before judges."
Ali indeed has his moments, but they are few. The most
effective occurs at the riot, when he is reduced from a man
of high moral dignity to a frightened boy. Ali will im-
partially save the life of a pagan as he has formerly saved
the life of the Christian Aissa, because it is a matter of
right; when he is struck down, he is so frightened that he
crawls away saying, 'Don't tell them—don't tell them.'
But Ali, sandwiched among some seventy characters in a
very short novel, is given little opportunity to become more
than a sketch for a portrait.

In *An American Visitor*, that uncomfortable juxtaposition
of violence and colloquy, the creative man is represented
not by an African but by the District Officer, Monkey
Bewsher. He is a reckless, enthusiastic man in his forties,
in love with the district over which he rules by the sheer
force of his personality; or rather, like Conrad's Kurtz, he is
in love with the power which he can exercise so freely in a
remote district of Nigeria. He is motivated by no disinterested benevolence: he treats the natives like naughty
children who must be subdued by the power of his imagination and the enlightenment of his superior knowledge. He
prefers that they remain subdued.

In order to maintain his dominance he must outsmart
not only the natives themselves but also the whites. He
subdues Marie Hasluck, the American newspaperwoman,
by communicating to her some of his own imaginative
vigour; and she succumbs so far as to become his mistress
and then his wife. He subdues the Governor by ignoring
his urgent orders. He subdues a party of prospectors,
despite their exclusive prospecting licence. 'There's no
reason on earth why they should come to Birri and smash
up my whole show.' He subdues, or tries to subdue, the

missioners by proposing, among other things, that the
pagan thunder god Ogun be transfigured into the Christian
saint of Electricity and Vital Energy.

But Bewsher is doomed, as are all megalomaniacs, to
defeat. He is killed by the very Africans over whom he has
ruled with such magnificent skill. Indeed before the fatal
battle he recognizes that there has come a term to his
sway. This is signalized by his willingness to shoot at the
Africans, whom formerly he has triumphed over without
force of arms. But Marie hides his pistol and he goes out
to meet them armed merely with a pair of scissors. And his
end has no tragic force. "Bewsher's own feelings as he lay
on the ground with two or three spears in his body, though,
of course, full of official indignation, was not empty of a
kind of amusement as if some part of his mind were
remarking to him, 'Well, old chap, the joke is on you.
You're not going to get away with it this time.'" How
near this is to the lightly uttered but equally despairing
remarks of Gulley Jimson when he and Nosy Barbon flee
in the rain to Sussex, toward the end of *The Horse's Mouth*.
How near and yet how far. For Gulley's vision is so much
more vast than Bewsher's megalomaniac dream; and
Gulley lives to begin, though not to finish, his last and
greatest painting.

In Cary's third novel, still another kind of man comes
to represent the creator. He is Louis Aladai, brother to the
African witch. Intelligent and well educated, his ambitions
are not for himself but for his people. He says to the lame
sometime don, Judith Coote, whom he knew in Oxford,
'Rimi civilization. Do you know what it is?—ju-ju.' He
tells Judith that no one, except a small handful, is educated
in Rimi. 'It's too absurd—a million without schools—and
Rimi civilization! Rimi! No, I love Rimi, and it is because

THE WORLD AS CHARACTER

I love it that I want to give it something worth calling a civilization.'

He soon discovers that there is nothing simple in the task of imposing European civilization upon his country-men, and he learns eventually that the call of his own culture is stronger than the call of Europe. Thus one of his supporters, the Reverend Selah Coker, is a Christian whom Louis despises. Coker's "key word was blood, but it appeared in different connections: blood of Jesus—blood of sacrifice—blood of the wicked man—blood of the sinner —the baptism of blood." All of Louis' civilized instincts are revolted by the man; and yet, near the end of the book when Coker has made a sacrifice of the Schweitzer-like Dr Schlemm and has put his head on display, Louis feels the power and the temptation of this emphasis in religion.

In fact he becomes confused, and his confusion is not resolved by the behaviour of most of the whites at Rimi. He longs for civilization, for good talk; and one night he joins the company of the whites, all of whom depart and leave him sitting alone—even Judith Coote leaves, having been summoned by her fiancé, Captain Rackham. The only person besides the Resident who treats him well on this occasion is, ironically, the athletic Dryas Honeywood, a girl whose reflexes cause her to be polite, but who in fact despises all the natives.

The die is cast late in the book during the crisis about the emirate. Tempers are frayed. In public and therefore specially humiliating circumstances, Captain Rackham, who regards Louis as a "trousered ape," the more despic-able because he has been educated, hits him and flings him into the river. When he is rescued, he is taken to his sister's house, where he orders Elizabeth to take his European clothes away and burn them. For, as he now says, 'I am

Rimi man.' And he is killed in the riot, or war, which his sister foments.

What Cary does in his first three novels, therefore, is to explore the possibilities of delineating the hero as creator, and he moves in the direction of complexity. That Ali becomes Bewsher and Bewsher becomes Louis Aladai indicates a progress in the development of this character, and it is a considerable achievement. But Cary's next novel, *Castle Corner*, fails just because complexity becomes diffuseness. The creator becomes several characters, all of them minor. Indeed, there are no major characters in this long and populous novel, intended, as Cary has said, to be the first volume of a trilogy.

In *Castle Corner* the free man appears in such fragmentary characters as John Charles Corner, whose entire artistry is expended—and charmingly but trivially expended—upon a tandem race from the castle to the village and back again; in Theodore Benskin, the South African millionaire; in Robert Porfit, an ambitious lay-preacher who appears briefly. Above all, this type is personated in Felix and Cleeve Corner, father and son.

Felix Corner, the elder son of the patriarch of Castle Corner, is a fine piece of satirical portraiture. Imposing in physique, devoted to talk, utterly foolish in his wisdom, "his good sense, his wide knowledge, almost as much as his imposing figure and large beard, his bass voice and spectacles, made him respected wherever he went." He has the temperament but not the single-mindedness of an artist. He lays waste his life in a number of footless schemes, the most absurd of which is his involvement in the Mosi Trading Company, a West African enterprise which he is certain will make all the Corners rich again. When Felix goes to Africa he writes utopian reports to

England, but before long he becomes entirely indolent and the Mosi Company becomes moribund. And so splendid is the ego of the man that when he is persuaded by his native concubine to marry his stepdaughter, he does not suppose that he is going native. In short, Felix Corner is an artist without an art, and this characterization, although it must dispel the idea that Cary is a yea-sayer, a devotee of progress, is simply not substantial enough to succeed in a book containing nearly a hundred characters.

Felix's son Cleeve is more interesting. His disorientation is more fundamental, because his mother and father have travelled incessantly round Europe, and so he has missed the security of a centre, of a home. Yet this very deracination allows him to develop in more fruitful ways than either Felix or John Chass, more fruitful also than the other two boys of his generation who play prominent rôles in the novel: his cousin, Cock Jarvis, who becomes a soldier; and Philip Feenix, a neighbour of the Corners whose surrender to the idea of landlordship involves a crucial surrender of freedom that drives him to suicide.

Having left his public school and returned to Ireland as he thinks for ever, Cleeve tries unsuccessfully to write a novel about a Roman youth called Manlius—he comes to feel that Castle Corner is a backwater. He longs for Oxford, for London, for the season, and he makes his escape, a very young young man hungry for experience of life. When at last Cleeve goes up to Oxford he attaches himself to a succession of styles all of which enable him to explore the shape of the world. He becomes first a dandy in imitation of his friend Cobden Chorley, then an ardent reader of philosophy, until he is carried—to his father's disquiet—beyond Kant who is the fashion to more controversial philosophical standpoints. Cleeve Corner is clearly

destined for a life in which intelligence will play a
commanding rôle, and there is every prospect that his
career will be more successful than his father's, for Cleeve's
liberation is not the half-way house of apostasy. But
whether Cleeve will fulfil his destiny is a question left un-
answered at the end of *Castle Corner*, the longest of Cary's
novels, and, paradoxically, the least developed.

Conscious of his failure, Cary returned to Africa for the
setting of his next novel, *Mister Johnson*, a little masterpiece owing its force to the brilliant simplicity with which
it is constructed. Arnold Kettle, in an excellent essay, calls
this book a lyric. *Mister Johnson* does indeed sing—and
principally through the characterization of that irresistible
young African, Johnson himself. In portraying Johnson,
Cary for the first time disclosed the scope of his great
novelistic talent.

The book begins with a falling in love which is for the
most part a construct of Johnson's lavish imagination, an
imagination nourished by his youthful and poetic experience of English civilization as he knows it through the
colonial officers for whom he works. "The young women
of Fada, in Nigeria, are well known for beauty. They have
small, neat features and their backs are not too hollow." So
begins this enchanting book, and Johnson falls in love with
Bamu the ferryman's daughter, not only because of her
beauty—'What pretty breasts—God bless you with them'
—but because he has dreams of grandeur. He will make
her into a government lady and in so doing will help to
complete his idea of himself as a government gentleman.
The relationship with Bamu is, however, less than half the
story; the other, more important relationship is between
Johnson and Harry Rudbeck, the Assistant District Officer.
He treats Johnson, "his first clerk, with the ordinary

politeness which would be given to a butler or footman at home," and Johnson adores him in return.

The pathos and humour of Johnson's position are indicated by its extreme precariousness, which is of course only a heightened version of the precariousness of the human situation anyway. Johnson has the capacity to forget which the reader is later to find in Sara Monday. His remorse, his despair—'Oh, Gawd, Oh, Jesus! I done finish—I finish now'—are real and agonized and short-lived. He immediately forgets his troubles when he starts to copy a report, for he delights in making capital S's. Indeed, Johnson's destiny becomes the more radiant as it becomes more uncertain. In difficulty with his creditors, he is charged with embezzlement. Furthermore, Bamu's brother, finding that Johnson cannot pay an instalment due on his sister, fetches her back to the ferry village. And, seeing the image of himself in the process of destruction, the boy gives himself to a suicidal despair. At last he is shown a way out of his difficulty: he becomes a paid spy for the Waziri. The rôle becomes possible, even desirable, because it is dangerous and therefore exhilarating. In order to get at the confidential files, Johnson must steal the key from underneath Rudbeck's pillow; when he has successfully done so, and when he has delivered to the Waziri the information desired, Johnson is so delighted with his new rôle as successful thief that he can hardly contain his joy.

So goes Johnson's splendid career from joy to sorrow and back again. It is a great piece of artistry; and, like all artistry, doomed in the very nature of things. His last great act is the greatest act of all, that of murder—it is a murder which he does not mean to undertake but which he is, in a way, trapped into committing. He kills Sergeant Gollup, who finds him stealing money from the cash-desk of

Gollup's store. And since Gollup is a white, there can be no question about Johnson's punishment.

His trial is a tragi-comedy, because Johnson, observing Rudbeck's kindness toward him, is cheerful, indeed exuberant, in giving testimony. Rudbeck puts together a statement, to which Johnson agrees—he would in his gratitude agree to anything—that the killing was unpremeditated. Johnson is, however, ordered to be hanged, and Rudbeck must do the hanging. Rudbeck feels so defiant, and so torn by friendship, that he does not, until pressed, execute the order. When he weighs Johnson, the young clerk guesses his fate. He begs Rudbeck to shoot him rather than hang him. 'Oh, say, you my good frien'—my father and my mother—I pray you do it—I tink perhaps you shoot me.' And this in fact is what Rudbeck does. He tells his wife Celia—it is the last line of the book—'I couldn't let any one else do it, could I.' It is a cry of anguish, a tragic awareness no less moving than Captain Vere's awareness in *Billy Budd* of the conflict between personal and public loyalty. But *Mister Johnson* is not Rudbeck's book; it is Johnson's. The young African's intense and endless imagining, his creation of a glorious destiny, require that we rejoice in his triumph while we lament his defeat.

In his characterization of Mister Johnson, Cary moves in a new direction: he explores the destructive as well as the creative aspect of the free man. I think it fair to say, in fact, that as his novels improve so his idea of the world matures. Cary can realize in art the shape of his world as the shape of the world clarifies itself in his own mind. Or it may be that in the act of creation itself Cary's world develops the shape which is a realization in both senses of the word. At any rate, from *Mister Johnson* onward the hero as creator is also, though in varying degrees, a rakehell: the *genres* of these artists vary, but each ruins himself for his art.

This is certainly true of Charley Brown, the cockney adolescent who is the hero of *Charley is My Darling*. His adventures in the village to which he has been evacuated are disastrous and destructive. He paints a picture in which he is the hero–adventurer; so compelling is the self-portrait that he is led from theft and burglary to the destruction of a great country house in his efforts to create a world. As an artist he is a failure because he, like Mister Johnson, is only half-educated to life's possibilities; but, like Mister Johnson, he learns of the route to community. It is the route of love, which Johnson feels toward Rudbeck, and which Charley Brown feels toward the deaf Lizzie Galor. At the end of the book, Charley escapes from a remand home and collects Lizzie. But they are caught by the police. Before they part, Lizzie says, 'It's bin so lovely, I wish I could die.' Indeed their parting is a little death, but it is not an annihilation: Charley Brown and Lizzie Galor have discovered separately because they have discovered together the bitter secret of human loneliness as they have discovered the sweet secret of human joy.

And in *Charley is My Darling* is Cary's first sketch of the man who is to become Gulley Jimson. In *Charley is My Darling* he is called Mr Lommax. He enchants the evacuees by his wild demeanour. When asked to conduct a drawing class for them, he reluctantly assents. 'Ah'll show em what it's about, if you like. But it won't do any good, you know, not a bit. They'll never learn anything. No one ever learns anything.' The boys are tantalized. As new-fledged leader of the gang, Charley explains that Mr Lommax 'aint a teacher, see, e's a real artiss.' And he continues to enchant. He is untidy and tardy and unconventional. He praises

Charley's drawings only when they become scatological.

When Charley is later put on trial for theft, Mr Lommax agrees to testify in his favour, for Charley is artistic. But, since Lommax thinks all children are artistic, it follows that he would testify for any other young miscreant. 'Can I say,' asks the earnest young woman in charge of the evacuees, 'that you think him promising as an artist?' To this Mr Lommax makes an altogether Jimsonian reply: 'Ah will come and swear it, if you like—perjury has no terrors for an artist—he is damned already.' In *Charley is My Darling*, however, Cary had not yet learned—at any rate, he did not attempt—to draw the shape of this damnation.

The other novel of childhood, *A House of Children*, is a special case just because it is autobiographical. The central figure is the narrator Evelyn Corner, writing of the time when he was eight years old. Evelyn is Cary's *alter ego*: but it is a measure of the difficulty of translating life to art that Cary invents another character, Harry, to bear a part of the burden of recollection. "I realized by some instinct (it was certainly not by reason) that the two together as a single character would be too complex for the kind of book I needed to write: a book full of that clarity, the large skies, and wide sea views, which belong to the vision of my childhood." Harry, the elder brother, the other aspect of Cary's *alter ego*, abandons art itself after the disastrous production of a play, a fact surely of great interest to those who would unlock the puzzle of Cary's own personality.

But Harry and Evelyn remain, at the end of the book, too young to have achieved even what Charley Brown achieves. Nevertheless, the free man appears in this book in the shape of Pinto, the holiday tutor, whose real name is actually Freeman. Pinto occupies a central position on the stage of their lives. Bored with teaching, quick-tempered, witty and imaginative, he appeals to their instinct to rebellion, their impulse to freedom. He speaks nonsense, which the children recognize as nonsense—for instance, "that policemen were the cause of crime and that the English had ruined India by stopping the widows from being burnt alive." But this nonsense is part of his sense, his shape of life. He is a utopian socialist, after William Morris; he is an artist and as artist anarchist, eternally at war with organization. He is interesting in this book not simply in himself but also as he prefigures Gulley Jimson.

There is, for instance, a simple rehearsal, in Pinto's story told against himself of pawning everything in a friend's flat, of Gulley Jimson's invasion of Sir William Beeder's flat. Pinto, the narrator tells us, "is an artist in description," and the story he tells is understatedly simple: "he described how he had been left to take care of a friend's, an artist's, rooms in London, but without money. The friend forgot to leave any and he had none. He therefore pawned a clock in order to telegraph for funds. But the telegram did not find its addressee, and no answer came. Meanwhile, according to Pinto, he had been obliged to pawn pictures, the cutlery, and at last the chairs and tables, till suddenly, while he was still hoping for funds to take everything out of pawn again, the friend himself had walked in and found him sleeping on a bare floor in the empty rooms."

The outline here follows almost exactly that of Gulley's occupation of Beeder's flat. But in *The Horse's Mouth* the incident is much elaborated. Gulley gets possession of the flat by a trick. He remains—for he is a real artist—to paint a wall, and he pawns all the furniture and fittings not so that he can eat, or rather not exclusively for this purpose, but so that he can paint. And when the owner returns, Gulley is sleeping on a floor, and must make an escape. While Pinto is "an artist in description," Gulley is an artist in fact.

After Pinto comes Gulley Jimson himself—Gulley at least as he is seen by Sara Monday; *A House of Children* and *Herself Surprised* were both published in 1941. And in the development of Gulley's character Cary delineates more fully than ever elsewhere his idea of man as creator, although in Chester Nimmo he embodies this idea with an impressiveness nearly equal to that of his realization in Gulley. These two characters, the heroes of the trilogies, must be treated separately, as the culmination of Cary's creative power, and they are the principal subject of the final chapter of this book. But I must say a word here about two works which were published between the two trilogies. They are *The Moonlight* and *A Fearful Joy*, both cast in the form of a chronicle, and each failing, as I have already suggested, for a different reason: *The Moonlight* because it has no central figure, *A Fearful Joy* because it attempts to chronicle too many of the revolutions in art and politics from the 1890s to the 1940s. These novels fail also, it seems to me, because they do not give Cary scope to explore the character of the free man. In *The Moonlight* there are only Geoffrey Tew, a young poet of the 'nineties who is an unsuccessful suitor of the romantic Ella Venn; and Ernest Cranage, somewhat weakly artistic in temperament, who is a science demonstrator and also Ella's seducer. The rôles of these two characters are very small. In *A Fearful Joy*, however, there is an important free man, the rogue Dick Bonser who is the heroine's tempter, seducer, husband and finally charge. He has, for Tabitha, real imaginative vigour. She cannot live without him, for

she comes to recognize the need in herself of the sheer
liveliness which he provides. At the end of the book, after
his death in a Paddington brothel—even after this—
Tabitha acknowledges what she owes the man. 'He
brought me to life again; it was like a resurrection from the
dead.' In fact, she reflects, Bonser, "that danger and
burden, has also been the ground and the sky of her life."
But Bonser, for all his pyrotechnics, plays a rôle in *A Fearful
Joy* altogether subordinate to that of Tabitha; and this, it
seems to me, is the wrong way round. Besides, Dick
Bonser's artistry consists neither in the creation of works
of art, like Gulley Jimson's paintings, nor in the creation
of a government, which is Chester Nimmo's political
ambition: Dick Bonser is a mere rogue, and after some
hundreds of pages he becomes to the reader, if not to
Tabitha, a bore.

3 *The Conservative Man*

Although Cary sets over against the free man another type
of character, the man attached to the past, to stability, to
achievement rather than to experiment—although Cary
does this, he is not simply juxtaposing opposites in order
to exalt the one and depress the other. Cary is, I think
without any question, on the side of the free man; but he
is extremely sympathetic to the gallery of conservatives
who people his novels. For, besides recognizing the fact
that this type exists, Cary acknowledges not only the
appeal but also the necessity of such a temperament in a
world blessed or doomed—'as you please'—with freedom.
Furthermore, he manages to show that these contrasting
characters are not opposite at every point. Even the most
rooted of Cary's conservatives must do battle in their own

souls with the impulse to create—and some of these characters actually do create, within certain limits. So Cock Jarvis in *Castle Corner* romps enthusiastically into a forbidden territory, and precipitates an international crisis. And the most fully realized of all the conservatives, Thomas Wilcher in the first trilogy, comes to acknowledge that creation and preservation, though always at war with each other, go hand in hand, willy-nilly.

Of course, it is true that all Cary's novels turn upon this war, but it is frequently fought out in terms that do not require the figuration of the conservative man. Thus *Aissa Saved* centres on the liberation—and this phrase is no tautology—of the free spirit, in religious terms. For Aissa this means a pull in opposite directions: toward her pagan lover Gajere and toward the Christianity taught by the missioners. But there does not appear in that novel any substantial character embodying the conservative spirit. Furthermore, Cary often chooses to dramatize his theme in the more purely Blakean terms of male versus female. *The Moonlight* and *A Fearful Joy* are both of them altogether too schematic in this dramatization. In *The Moonlight* it is Rose who resists, and Ella who succumbs to, the creative impulse; in *A Fearful Joy* Tabitha repeatedly comes to recognize that she cannot live without the rascally Bonser; and he for his part always returns to her because she offers his creative spirit a completion equally necessary.

But in the best of the novels—in *Mister Johnson* and the two trilogies—the conservative character plays a prominent rôle. Indeed, there are two kinds of conservatives in the canon, and each is given an ultimate characterization in the trilogies. There is the conservative by intellectual and spiritual commitment figured in the lawyer Thomas

92

Wilcher, and there is the conservative by instinct figured
in the soldier Jim Latter. But the lines cross; these are not
pure types worked out according to a grand preliminary
plan. They are, on the contrary, discovered in the course
of writing a number of novels. In Cary's early work I find
sketches and half-portraits of these conservatives.

There is, first of all, Harry Gore in *An American Visitor*,
an intellectual who has found his way to Africa. Nick-
named the Stork "because of his long thin legs, his long
neck and long face and long beak," he resembles even in
physique the character who is to become, ten years later,
Thomas Wilcher. Gore's rôle as a colonial officer is to
forestall, mediate and arrange. Everyone else in the book
is passionately committed to a positive course of action:
Marie Hasluck to militant pacifism, Monkey Bewsher to
assertion of his authority, the prospectors to pressing their
claims, the Africans to maintaining their authority and
identity. Harry Gore's rôle is simply preventive. In order
to keep the peace he lends Marie money, attempts to maintain intercourse between Bewsher and the prospectors,
urges the prospectors to press their claims tactfully, and
endeavours to avoid a war between blacks and whites.
Gore is accused by one of the prospectors of playing at life,
and so thoroughly does he understand the other man's
nature that he rather sympathizes with the prospector. At
the end of the book he realizes that all his management has
not prevented alteration in the status quo. He becomes
gloomy and pessimistic. "For Gore the world was going
to the devil. A new dark age of persecution, superstition,
tyranny and general wretchedness impended. Glory and
loveliness stood on their last legs." And thenceforward the
book becomes a kind of essay by Cary on the necessity of
recognizing the fact that the world is always in a state of

revolution. *An American Visitor* becomes a thesis and thus ceases to be a novel. And what is interesting in a man like Gore is not so much what leads up to his disillusionment as what afterwards impends. Perhaps, therefore, it was necessary for Cary to write Harry Gore into a novel before he could make him into Thomas Wilcher.

The other conservative—the soldier who becomes at his best Wilcher's loyal and simple-minded brother, Bill, at his worst the paranoid Jim Latter of the second trilogy—is prefigured variously in the early novels. The first appearance of this man is in *The African Witch* in the person of Captain Rackham, a young Irishman who is Assistant Police Commissioner in the Nigerian district of Rimi. He is full of gaiety, bounce and charm. He has an old-fashioned devotion to duty and he closes his mind to the political movement in Nigeria. He supposes his duty to consist in maintaining British supremacy in the colony, and he therefore resents such a man as the claimant to the Rimi throne, Louis Aladai. Rackham, indeed, flings him ignominiously into the river. This act spells the end of Rackham's career, the end of his engagement to Judith Coote and the end of his residence in Africa. The narrator tells of the young man's departure for England, where he is to keep a training stable in Berkshire; and there surely he will become, though the book does not say so, embittered for the same reasons that Jim Latter becomes embittered when he retires from Africa. To see in Rackham an early version of Jim Latter is to be reminded of the sympathy which Cary would invoke even for that murderous man. For Rackham is not unattractive; his very real quality is indicated in the nature of his response to the lame and sensitive Judith Coote, to whom he is for a time betrothed.

In *Castle Corner* both kinds of conservative appear—the

soldier in Cock Jarvis, the intellectual in Philip Feenix. Jarvis's destiny is that of empire-builder. From a boy he displays the soldierly virtues of solemnity, reckless courage, simple patriotism. When he is infatuated with a seventeen-year-old girl, he takes long walks with her, in the course of which he expatiates upon "the ruin of the world and the need for loyalty and self-sacrifice to save it." For Jarvis is a romantic. "To see an old custom die was for him like seeing an old and glorious hero leave the world; and to feel deprived of that glory." His career, therefore, has a certain splendour. As an enthusiastic officer in the West African Frontier Force, he subscribes to what the narrator calls "the master faith of the age; the idea of the struggle for existence; the survival of the fittest; the idea that some power in nature itself, a scientific providence discovered and proved by Darwin, had ordained progress by universal war." It is thus perfectly natural that he should, against government orders and against private orders, invade the Daji emirate, and thus precipi-tate an international crisis. His enterprise requires not only great daring but great endurance. But his spirit is invincible, and his soldierly intelligence superb. And though no one knows how to take the news of his victory, he comes back to England a hero: his triumph coincides with the Boer agitation, and chauvinism is the style of the hour.

But since the *Castle Corner* trilogy remains unfinished, Harry Jarvis's career is not fully detailed. The career of Philip Feenix, however, is interrupted by suicide at the end of *Castle Corner* itself. Son of a colourless Protestant clergyman and nephew of a domineering and doting uncle, he is doomed to the mere pathos of mere failure. Tied by the strings of responsibility and love to his dynamic uncle,

James Slatter, he surrenders again and again his chances for freedom. His uncle intends him to possess Castle Corner, and for years awaits the opportunity to take it over from John Chass, so that he can give it to his beloved Philly. But the opportunity never comes, and in the meantime Philip passes by the opportunity to go to Cambridge, or to go away from Ireland and become a missioner. He acts as Slatter's agent and secretary, and without knowing the cause of his dissatisfaction with life, turns to drink, lethargy and finally torpor.

His last chance is to marry his cousin Constance, and the account of their wedding journey to London is deeply touching. The couple are accompanied by Slatter, who by refusing his nephew money hopes to keep him sober. On their first night in London there is a moving scene between the embittered groom and the loving bride. She offers to get drink for her husband. 'Aw, Philly,' she says, 'I'd do anything to make ye happy.' She does get him drink, and it mollifies him. "He drank with great dignity, sitting at the dressing table, and as he raised the tooth glass to his lips, he said, 'Not that I need the beastly stuff, but why shouldn't I have it.' He looked grandly at Coo, who had crept quietly into bed. 'This won't save you.'" But Philip remains a drunk, and at last in a rage of despair he kills himself.

In *Mister Johnson* there are two conservatives, Harry Rudbeck and Sergeant Gollup. I have said enough about Rudbeck, who is, like Gollup, only lightly sketched out: for the book is almost altogether Johnson's. But Gollup must be dealt with here. He is an old soldier, a cockney with a sense of order who has built a good business in Fada. He is a man with a murderous temper, but he quickly forgets his anger. He likes Johnson, and the boy, perceiving this, likes him in return. Besides, Gollup is a man of imagination. On Sunday afternoons he gets drunk and becomes a philosopher. He talks about England and the regiment. "Gollup has the usual hatred of the old soldier for the rich and their women, and in fact for all those who live easy and self-indulgent lives without risk or responsibility, that hatred which has made all countries with conscription inclined to violent revolution." He is an empire man, a sort of working-class Jim Latter whose passionate luridness Johnson responds to without understanding it.

Finally—for the novels of childhood do not deal with the conservative temper except as it is potential in the children themselves—there are the conservatives in the two trilogies. In the Thomas Wilcher of the first trilogy (complemented by his soldier brother) and in the James Latter of the second are the penultimate embodiments, and they are first-rate characterizations altogether. But the ultimate embodiment is Chester Nimmo, who in the course of his career is transmogrified from the free to the unfree man: so tantalizing, so difficult, and so repellent that Cary tried in *The Moonlight* and *A Fearful Joy* to do without this kind of man. He did not fully succeed, for the life-defeated James Groom of *The Moonlight* and the life-defeated son of Tabitha in *A Fearful Joy* belong to this type. But partly because they are sketchy, the books are sketchy. Cary's map of the world requires a map in depth of the conservative man. Such a map is to be found in Wilcher, in Latter and in Nimmo.

4 *The Female*

In every single one of Cary's novels there is a woman of impressive moral stature—impressive because she recognizes by instinct if not by ratiocination a rôle in life of some considerable magnitude. Generally, the moral stature of these women is matched by physical bulk, the outward and visible sign of their specially female grace. And all of them possess the splendid vigour which stems from certainty. This is not to say that they are unperplexed. Indeed—to take the most complex of them all—Nina in the second trilogy becomes from time to time so perplexed that she tries to take her own life: she becomes perplexed just because she is so certain that her rôle in life is to be Chester Nimmo's spouse, and she can hardly bear it. Above all, the Cary heroines exist not independently but dependently— upon the men whom it is their destiny to cherish; and when, as in *The Moonlight*, female sexuality is denied, the female nature becomes contorted. Cary draws women well. His skill derives in part, I think, from his thoroughly masculine comprehension of what is, despite all emancipation, still the opposite sex. In fact, Cary's women are often better than his men.

So it is Aissa who saves *Aissa Saved*: she who redeems it from mediocrity, she who makes it a first novel of promise. Among the central figures in Cary's novels, Aissa is certainly the simplest. Less educated even than the Ali who was originally meant to be the hero of this novel, Aissa is neither so intelligent as the Elizabeth of *The African Witch* nor so sophisticated as the almost entirely unsophisticated Sara Monday. Aissa's character can be drawn only in bold relief, because she is elemental; and she is therefore no doubt an excellent choice for the heroine of a first novel. Her ultimately fatal effort to create a life out of the materials given her is recorded with Cary's altogether characteristic sympathy for the human impulse to love, to create, to fulfil.

THE WORLD AS CHARACTER

Aissa's devotion to Christianity springs initially from gratitude: she has come to the Shibi Mission as a refugee from her native village, and she makes Christianity into a substitute for what she has already discovered by instinct to be the foundation of her life: Christ becomes the father of her child and even, as she supposes when she is taking the sacrament of the Lord's supper, her husband. Such perplexity as she often feels is instantly resolved when surrogate and actuality meet: Aissa breaks off her singing of a hymn when she spies her husband Gajere, and she runs to his embraces. Nor will she return to the mission while she and Gajere can be together. Much of her life is spent protecting her child, who is more important to her than belief, more important than life itself. Toward the end of the book, reunited with Gajere after a long separation and after a number of scarifying experiences, Aissa asserts very practically, 'I do plenty good for Jesus. . . . Jesus, he do plenty for me. Good-bye now—all done finish.' But when, having been dragged off to the ants' nest to die, she is forever separated from Gajere, she turns to Jesus again, as substitute husband. "Jesus . . . had taken her, he was carrying her away in his arms."

The heroine of *An American Visitor* is, though extremely ignorant and naïve, more sophisticated than Aissa. Marie Hasluck, the American visiting Nigeria, is an anarchist; she has a faith, but it is an educated faith. As a newspaperwoman who has come to Africa to write a series of articles on native culture, she wishes to substantiate her prejudices in favour of what she takes to be noble savagery; and the book is a record both of her disillusionment in this respect and of her discovery of a faith differently based, a faith based on a truer apprehension of her own nature and thus of human nature altogether. At the beginning she is thought to be 'a very dangerous agitator.' This is because, as one of the prospectors explains, she is 'teaching self-determination to bare-arsed apes.' Another replies that if he 'was an Amurcan girl brought up on Freud and the fourteen points mixed in with Valentino and turned loose in a wilderness of notion salesmen and ward politicians, he'd be Bolshy. But the fact was that the poor bitch didn't know what she was or what she wanted. That was the trouble.' This is indeed Marie's trouble, although she does not discover the fact for some considerable time. At first, and despite evidence to the contrary from the beginning, she reads Africa through the eyes of Rousseau.

The common ground which Marie and Monkey Bewsher find is a mutual distrust of civilization. For different reasons each dislikes the idea of the "encroachment" of civilization upon native culture. On the evening after both of them have nearly been killed by the natives, they argue with Frank Cottee, one of the prospectors, while Gore attempts to make conciliatory remarks to both parties. Cottee attacks Marie as an anarchist, and Marie is secretly frightened; she "was liable to these fits of doubt and dreaded them. They had a physical effect upon her nerves. She felt sometimes as if the actual ground had wavered and sunk beneath her. It was for a moment as if the most solid objects were illusory, as if there was nothing secure, nothing fixed, permanent and trustworthy in the whole world; no peace, no refuge."

There is indeed no refuge in the beliefs which she has brought as baggage to Africa with her. But she finds her way confusedly and certainly to the female destiny of wife to Bewsher; and shedding the impedimenta of anarchism she attaches herself to him in such domestic dependence that she can as easily dispense with ungrounded faith as

Aissa herself. It is not simply the facts of Africa that over-turn Marie Hasluck's beliefs: it is the overwhelming fact of female life.

With his customary daring, Cary makes Elizabeth Aladai, the African witch, the moral centre of his third novel. Tall, bulky, strong, this woman of "monumental dignity" is a ju-ju priestess and she dominates *The African Witch*: dominates her brother Louis Aladai; dominates Judith Coote, the lame and lively don who has come to Nigeria because she is engaged to the equally lively though not so talented Assistant Police Commissioner Jock Rackham; dominates the Reverend Selah Coker, whose idea of Christianity centres on sacrifice; dominates the Mohammedan claimant to the throne—and even causes the most powerful white man in the area, the Resident, to walk several miles because she has declared a woman's war.

Her first appearance is especially impressive. She comes to the door of her ju-ju house and "she almost filled the opening which framed her with sunlight streaming into the yard behind. She was a woman who seemed, in her height and proportions, bigger than the largest and most powerful men. In fact she was probably about five foot ten in height, and fifteen or sixteen stone in weight—not of fat, but of bone and muscle." She conducts a trial to decide why the babies of a local woman become sickly and die. Having listened to the evidence, she gives herself to the ju-ju spirit, "and now she felt that spirit swelling and spreading through her whole body. She released her muscles—her arms hung like bags of lead on the aching hands of the girl —she softened her legs, bending them at the knees, making her flesh soft for the penetration of the spirit." At last she fixes upon a girl named Osi. When Osi says she has no ju-jus, Elizabeth orders fire to be put to her.

Elizabeth is powerful not only in her own realm, the ju-ju house and its surroundings, but within the entire purview of the novel. *The African Witch*'s plot turns on a struggle for the succession to the emirate of Rimi. The two chief contenders for the throne are a Mohammedan leader named Salé and Elizabeth's brother Louis, who is a Christian. Since Salé's accession would threaten her because it threatens ju-ju, she supports her brother's claims, not because he tolerates ju-ju, but because he is "a fool boy. She could manage Aladai at any time."

Elizabeth's greatest triumph is the women's war, of which she is instigator and commanding general. She undertakes it because she wishes to support her brother's royal claims. At one point she is saved by her female nature. She is captured and imprisoned. When she refuses bribes, her captors feed her poisoned chicken and put her into a hole in the bush to be eaten by hyenas. In such circumstances a more ordinary mortal would die. But not Elizabeth. She is rescued, taken back to her compound, and delivered of a baby. Before long the women's war is resumed, and although it is brought to an end quickly when the troops are called out by the Resident, Elizabeth herself is not defeated. Indeed she has her most complete triumph of all when her paramour Akande Tom, who has tried to escape from her and who is attempting with the help of Judith Coote to "learn book," returns to her in misery and terror. Elizabeth works her ju-ju on him and he crawls to her on all fours. He is whipped "and he no longer tries to be a white man, or to learn book."

Elizabeth Aladai is perhaps the most stunning of Cary's females, and female she is. She is woman triumphant rather than woman subdued. She acts out the rôle described in "The Mental Traveller," for she binds iron thorns around

the heads of her men, and conquers them. Because she is
stronger than any of the men within her orbit she succeeds
to fail: the process described in Blake's poem requires a
man to rend up his manacles. Elizabeth, therefore, is Sara
Monday or Nina Nimmo victorious; the two English-
women are luckier in that the material with which they
have to work is adamant, and so their female destinies are,
paradoxically, more thoroughly fulfilled in submissiveness.

Castle Corner and the two novels of childhood mark a
transition, it seems to me, from the starkness of Africa to
the complexities of the English scene depicted in *The
Moonlight*, *A Fearful Joy* and the two trilogies. I am
arrested in *Castle Corner* by the figure of Helen Pynsant,
the not altogether respectably fashionable woman who is in
a way a sketch for the Tabitha of *A Fearful Joy*, although
Helen is a colder and less sympathetic figure. In *Charley is
My Darling* there is Lizzie Galor, the adolescent girl to
whom Charley becomes attached, a girl whose devotedness
is as deep and instinctive and complete as that of every
other Cary heroine. And there is in *A House of Children* the
general favourite Delia, a sixteen-year-old girl the very
violence of whose personality grips the imagination. "Even
when she was sitting still, she had the air of intense
activity within; of rapid and concentrated thought or
vigorous feeling or both." Against her the phlegmatic
Frances, who marries early and respectably and not for
love but for motherhood, is a fine contrast. But none of
these females is realized in the transitional novels as well as
they are elsewhere.

In *The Moonlight* female nature is the very subject. The
intended commanding centre of the book is Miss Ella Venn,
the seventy-four-year-old younger sister of Rose and the
mother (though this fact is not acknowledged until quite

late in the book) of Amanda. It is a happy choice of viewpoint. For Ella both as younger sister and as mother is a
mediator between the generations. Rose as a Victorian
lives for duty; Amanda as a child of the twentieth century
lives in the atmosphere of emancipation; and Ella, who
understands female nature better than either of them, tries
to reconcile both her sister and her daughter to a more
accurate version. Ella is inarticulate—she is supposed by
her relations to be a romantic—but she has that splendid
vitality and instinctive commitment to female nature so
characteristic of Cary heroines. The book fails not because
of the rôle of Ella Venn but because of faults of construction
and viewpoint: because, as a thesis-novel in answer to a
thesis-novel, it forgets to be novel at all.

Of Tabitha Baskett in *A Fearful Joy* nearly enough has
already been said. The daughter of a suburban doctor, she
is "a small thin girl with large, too prominent eyes, a
thick mouth, a snub nose, and a heavy clubbed pigtail of
brown hair. And she was still remarkable for nothing but
a certain violence of ordinariness." After her father's death
Tabitha becomes severely and perfervidly religious. She is
devoted to her elder brother Harry "because she knew that
he was good;" he is not an affectionate man and he lectures
her; but she hates his wife Edith—"handsome, sensual,
rather blowsy, fond of bright colours and rich food, critical,
like a woman much loved, of her husband." Tabitha embraces the idea of being a missioner in China, until a
missioner dares criticize ladies who ride bicycles. She
then determines to become a concert pianist, and practises
six hours a day for over a year. But she becomes restless.
She says to herself, 'Oh—oh—oh, if only something would
happen!'

At once—in consonance with the rules of melodrama—

she becomes involved with Dick Bonser, the handsome young man who has been black-balled from the local tennis club; who is in debt, but who expects a large inheritance as soon, he says, as a law case is decided in his favour. Bonser tells her fascinating things about himself—for instance, that he is the illegitimate son of "a nobleman of the highest rank and a countess." He declares great love for Tabitha and a few days after proposes marriage to her. Tabitha cannot say no, and she runs away with him.

Such is the beginning of Tabitha's first adventure with Bonser, and it establishes the pattern of all the others. She is drawn to him irresistibly from girlhood because of the radiance and the fertility of his imagination. The duplicity in his character, the bombast of his speech, the fatuousness of his grandiose schemes eternally madden her, but throughout the course of her life she is vitalized in spirit by this restless, roguish, animated man. Even after he dies at a great age, the memory of the man, and the reincarnation of his spirit in his granddaughter by Tabitha, renew the old woman's life.

Cary's vision is tripartite, and the three figures on the landscape of his world require one another. When, as in *The Moonlight* and *A Fearful Joy* the female dominates, the whole picture becomes inadequate because distorted. The men of *The Moonlight* never come forward—or if they do they are soon made to beat a retreat before the person and then the ghost of Rose Venn. Nor can Dick Bonser take his place in *A Fearful Joy*; the book is too thoroughly Tabitha's, and he has no complement as do both Gulley Jimson and Chester Nimmo. But Sara and Nina are both torn between the free and the unfree man, which is simply to say that their complicated female natures demand a complexity, in fact a contradiction, in response. Sara and

Nina succeed as characters by virtue of their relationships. They succeed also—and this is perhaps putting the same matter in other words—because they can tell their own stories, which can be corrected in their turn by the stories of their men.

To notice, as I have been doing in this chapter, how often Cary repeats himself, is not, I trust, to suggest by way of derogation that he is a limited writer. Limited he surely is—and so is everyone else by culture, temperament, intelligence, experience. Cary differs, as all artists differ, from other people in coming to have a sense of the scope of his limitation. And he differs also in that the richness of his culture, the sturdiness of his temperament, the acuity of his intelligence, the catholicity of his experience made possible the writing of novels representing something worth representation. What I have been saying in this chapter shows something else as well: that the literary artist's endeavour is not simply to work with the variously tractable medium of language and the variously tractable medium of structure. The artist's endeavour must be to know himself. When Cary achieved this knowledge— indeed it is no doubt more accurate to say that he came to know himself through coming to terms with his art—he could write the trilogies. These are the subject of the following chapter.

CHAPTER FOUR

The Inevitable Style

1 *Prospect*

CARY'S prose style is readily distinguishable and often distinguished, but it does not altogether perfect itself until, in *A House of Children* and the two trilogies, style becomes the man or the woman narrating the story being told. In his own person Cary's style is remarkable on account of a constant employment of the word "drunk" ("Sometimes they laughed so much that they appeared to be drunk," he writes in *An American Visitor*, for instance), the iteration of which suggests the frenzy that Cary believes to be the major mode of human life. In the same way the historical present tense, which he uses so often, suggests not merely the immediacy but also the furor of the fact of living. There is also the syntactic anticlimax which by its very irony coruscates, so that Aissa's horrifying fate, to be eaten alive by ants, is set down with Swiftian objectivity: the ants "were especially eager to get food for their community." Altogether, Cary's is the plain style of a man in a hurry who thinks the world is in a hurry; it is the style of a man who must explain the world to itself.

Nor are his characters often in repose. Even those who think deeply are hardly shown being given opportunity to reflect calmly or continuously. They are forever being interrupted by riots, strikes, murders, wars, elections, insults, bankruptcies, crumbling buildings, or summonses for indecent exposure. The prevailing tone of all the novels

is one of agitation. This is not because Cary believed that
man is always agitated but because he believed that agitation is always imminent and that in agitation man
characteristically reveals himself. Cary knew, indeed, that
a novel is not a slice of life but a portrait from which much
must be omitted if it is to tell the truth. "Cary's method,"
he quotes an American critic as saying, "is to put a
character in a jam and see how he fares." This is not the
method so much as it is the situation of all the characters
in all the novels. As a generalization it is, Cary says, "true
as far as it goes—and therefore misleading. It overlooks
the point that for me all characters are in a jam, all of us
are in a jam, a special and incurable difficulty from which
there is no escape. It continues all our lives and affects
every aspect of our existence—we are born to freedom
in a world condemned to be free, for its own good, for its
own maintenance and for its own destruction."

But in the attempts to mediate between action and
audience, Cary's style breaks down. It is a familiar predicament, familiar at least since the eighteenth century, when
writers began to have mixed audiences. The remarkable
fact about Cary is the comparative ease which he exhibits
in his relation to his readers, whom he supposes to be
cultivated but somewhat provincial Oxford. It is, however,
only a comparative ease. "Gossip is the major pastime of
Africa," he says in *An American Visitor*. "All books are
magic and sacred objects in Yanrin where no one knows
how to read them," he writes in *Aissa Saved*. Such inter-
positions are common enough in the African novels, but
they are almost as common in the novels whose settings
are, though within the United Kingdom, presumed to be
outside the experience of the Oxford reader. Thus in *Castle
Corner* and *A House of Children* Cary explains Ireland to his

audience. "A starer in Annish is much feared," he writes in the first of these novels; in the other the whole intent is, in explaining an Irish childhood to himself, to give the experience a communicable status. Even *Charley is My Darling*, set in Devon, requires explanation, because Oxford has to be told about the impact of the cockney upon the west. "They did not know that hi, Bill, wait for me Sunday, which had been an invitation, was now a threat, or that the answer, I'll be seeing ya, was a defiance. In London, both these speeches, uttered in the same tone, would have brought instant inquiries to know if there was going to be a fight and where it might be found." Nor can Cary always resist the temptation to *épater l'Oxford*. Of Aissa's love for her child he writes: "Devoted mothers are as common in Kolu as elsewhere. That kind of love is a natural thing, as cheap as air and water, and common to cats, bitches and hyenas." Of dancing in Nigeria he declares, in *The African Witch*: "For real dancers, like Rimi people, dancing like poetry is a communication as well as an expression. They speak in the movements of the body not only of passion, but tenderness, sympathy—such as an Englishman may feel and think he expresses while he treads on his partner's toes."

But when Cary can impersonate his narrator he can—as Henry Reed points out in *The Novel Since* 1939—eliminate himself. He can suit the words to the character so justly that in the novels of the two trilogies there are six styles: six metaphorical structures, six schemes of syntax, six kinds of interior monologue—indeed, six worlds. They clash. But that these worlds constitute different aspects of a single world, and that this world has a "final" shape is a fact clearly to be drawn from a consideration of each of the trilogies as a whole. To write a novel in the first person may be to hide behind the mask of the narrator; to write trilogies of the kind now to be discussed is, on the other hand, to insist upon "finality," for the reader is constantly required to compare and assess the versions of the same world presented by competent but interested witnesses. The reader is forced to draw a final conclusion, by himself.

2 The First Trilogy

However different they may be in other respects—and surely three more sharply contrasted characters could hardly be found than the voluptuous cook who is Sara Monday, the conservative lawyer who is Thomas Wilcher and the rebellious artist who is Gulley Jimson—the narrators of the first trilogy have in common the fact of imprisonment. Sara of *Herself Surprised* is writing her memoirs in jail for a hundred pounds, with which she will pay Gulley's and his son Tommy's bills; the penny-press is enabling her to make a virtue of the necessity of her imprisonment, and permitting her even there to fulfil what she conceives to be her rôle in life. Wilcher of *To be a Pilgrim* is, throughout his book, virtually committed to Tolbrook, the house which has always been the prison of his life anyway; his bondage is not more real, it is only more obvious than ever. And Gulley of *The Horse's Mouth* emerges from prison at the beginning of his book; at the end, he is mortally ill in a police ambulance. As politics is the basic metaphor of the second trilogy, so imprisonment is the root situation of the first. Sara, a comic character in a tragic world, is trapped between the claims of her feminine moral sense and society's moral code. Wilcher, a tragic figure because he can perceive the anatomy of his entrapment, is caught between the claims of past and present. Gulley, also tragic, is imprisoned between the claims of self and the claims of the institution—any institution, all institutions. But Sara, Wilcher and Gulley are also, and this is simply putting the matter another way, imprisoned in their own subjectivities. They are, like Snow the cat at the end of *The Horse's Mouth*, irremediably isolated. For to be free is to be alone; to be alone is to be imprisoned: freedom's lonely bondage is, in the first trilogy as always in Cary, the tragic fact of a tragic world.

It is therefore a paradox, but it is no contradiction, that these volumes have in common also a comic lavishness unknown in the English novel since Dickens. Cary is no joyful trout, if by that phrase sheer acceptance of life is implied; but he is able to delight in the splendour and the sordidness of man's very manhood, and thus to express his own sense of triumph over the world's idiocy. Dickens himself was no yea-sayer: and his best novels are informed by the sense of the senselessness, of the injustice, of the malevolence, which underlie human motivation. This is simply to say that tragedy and comedy do not merely go hand in hand; they are very often bedfellows.

Sara, like Gulley, belongs to the picaresque tradition—the sturdiest and in many ways the most centrally novelistic of fictional methods. That sixteenth-century picaro, Lazarillo de Tormes, is in constant friction with the society of which he is a part. But, as Professor Castro points out, he is no revolutionary. Indeed he embraces, he celebrates, the life which he is lucky enough to be able to live. And the whole of his book is a boast of his triumph. The convention of the journey in the picaresque novel does permit this celebration, this triumph, this boast in various circumstances and in different places. Within the English novelistic tradition, the nearest book to *Herself Surprised* is *Moll*

111

Flanders. The books do have in common a narrative device, a self-justifying heroine and a series of adventures. They have also in common a rejoicing. But it is easy to go too far. Moll Flanders is a filcher, delighting in her own filchings; Sara is a prisoner of her own kind of grace, delighting in her rôle in life, which is that of housekeeper to the various men with whom she becomes involved. If the symbol of Moll's life can be said to be money—and preferably money illicitly got—the symbol of Sara's life is certainly the kitchen. This fact is made plain by the associative structure of her reflections. "The sun was as bright as a new gas mantle—you couldn't look at it even through your eyelashes, and the sand as bright-gold as deep-fried potatoes. The sky was like washed-out Jap silk, and there was just a few little clouds coming out on it like down feathers out of an old cushion; the rocks were as warm as new gingerbread cakes and the sea had a melty thick look, like oven glass." But Sara has also a sense of womanhood which makes her have much more in common with the Wife of Bath and with Dame Quickly than with Moll Flanders, who hardly appreciates the joys of the female flesh. "I designed Sara as the inveterate nest builder," Cary said in a letter, "and I don't think you could imagine anyone further than that from Defoe's old bawd."

The title *Herself Surprised* does of course work in both the directions which the richness of the English language permits. Sara is surprised at herself, surprised to find herself doing what she does. "At first," she says, "I could not believe that I was anything like the woman they made me out to be." She is wonder-struck at the picture drawn of her in the courtroom. But because of the narrative device— she is telling her own story—she is also surprised by the reader in the act of living. The reader, like Sara, is breathless, though not for the same reason. Sara is writing against time. She must finish her confession while she is still news; no doubt the "kind gentleman . . . from the news agency" is chivvying her. And she wants the hundred pounds which she is being paid, because she has been "fretting for our quarter day." But the celerity of the pace conveys also the vigour of Sara's character. Sara, unlike Wilcher and Gulley, does not reflect. She lives, even more obviously than they do, by her feelings, which are generous, catholic and strong. The Biblical Sarah baked bread for her guests, was praised by Peter for submissiveness to her husband, and bore a son at the age of ninety-one. As an old woman, "Sarah laughed within herself, saying, After I am waxed old shall I have pleasure?" (Genesis 18, 12).

The judge who sentences Sara to prison calls her 'a woman without any moral sense,' and he has come to this conclusion because 'several times during the gravest revelations of her own frauds and ingratitude, Mrs Monday smiled.' Sara herself comes to believe, to a certain extent and in a certain way, this objective view. But the book exists, for the reader more than for Sara, to explore the tension between the official and the human versions of her life. Sara's enjoinder is that "some who read this book may take warning and ask themselves before it is too late what they really are and why they behave as they do." As is suitable in a newspaper confession story and at the same time conformable to her own nature, piety is writ large. She claims to know herself for the first time in her life, but she does not. In the end is her beginning, all over again. On the last page of the book she comforts herself: "A good cook will always find work, even without a character, and can get a new character in twelve months, and better herself, which God helping me, I shall do, and keep a more watchful eye, next time, on my flesh, now I know it better." Sara remains true to her own nature, but this is not to say that she lacks a moral sense. Her very physique—she is a big, fleshy, healthy country girl—suggests a moral stature of some considerable force. Her response, inexpressible by herself, is to a morality far deeper than the Victorian code to which she subscribes: it is the morality of Eve.

The first of the men to whom she becomes attached, the sturdily middle-class and entirely unprepossessing Matthew Monday, demonstrates this morality. Sara calls it Nature. Thus, although she does not even like him very much, she yields to his proposal that they marry. And though she is much surprised at herself, she acknowledges the inevitability of an inevitable Nature. She goes further: she accommodates herself to her rôle as Mrs Matthew Monday—even, indeed, to the extent of falling in love with him. "No girl could have helped loving a man so kind in himself and so loving to her."

For he is the most pliable of what Gulley Jimson calls her "victims." She teaches him to make love confidently and so improves his self-esteem. She persuades him to play golf and entertain his friends. She helps him to become a town councillor. She bears him several children. That is to say, the nest she builds for Matthew Monday is serenely Victorian; it conforms to her view of the Happy Home drawn from Victorian novels. Sara is content with this life for a number of years, but she would cease to be Sara if she were simply to settle forever into the routine of respectability. Her own vitality requires vitality of response; by instinct she seeks renewal and refreshment. Therefore, when the down-and-out artist Gulley Jimson comes to undertake a painting for the town council, she is drawn to this man even to the extent of disobeying her husband by posing for him.

Gulley is "the most of a man I ever knew:" if he gives Sara more sorrow he also gives her more joy than any of the other men to whom she becomes attached. After Matt dies, Sara goes off with him and lives with him as Mrs Jimson, although they cannot marry because Gulley may still have a wife. Sara's new relationship stands in sharp contrast to her marriage with Matthew Monday, but it is not only that the man is different, it is also that Sara has learned some lessons about life. She has learned to savour her rejoicings. Her happiness with Gulley, when they are on their honeymoon—for so she calls it—at Bournemouth, is the deeper for being more self-conscious. Not that she really understands Gulley. "All he wants," she decides on seeing his joy at Bournemouth, "is a little success and respect and money, which is every man's right, to ease his mind and take it off the stretch and please God he will have it now." This is at once her strength and her weakness in her relationship to Gulley. For she can give him ease and peace. She can take care of him. She can rejoice with him in the pleasure of the flesh. But between mind and mind there is no communication. Gulley cannot discuss art with Sara, for to Sara art is pretty pictures—the sort which hung in the morning room at Matt's house, and which Gulley caused to be removed. Nor does she understand his religion, though she reports what he says. 'You're Mrs Em and I'm Gulley Jimson and that fly on the wall has its own life too—as big as it likes to make it, and it's all one to God as the leaves to the tree.' Gulley chides Sara for going to early service, because she is making religion into a self-punishment. Nor, finally, does Sara understand Gulley's politics, which are pure anarchism.

115

In fact, Gulley comes to feel oppressed by Sara's management of himself. 'Do you know, Sall,' he says in anger
against himself and therefore against her, 'I wish the
very name of artist was abolished. It's simply a bad smell,
it's not even good English. Painter is the English word,
or limner. Well, I'm a working painter. Tell me what
to paint and I'll paint it.' This is Gulley talking not only
angrily but wishfully. For nothing is less true than that
he can paint to order. Indeed, orders, management—or,
as he calls it—nagging, stop him completely. That is
why in agonized frustration he hits Sara on the nose. She
cannot apprehend, as the reader must infer, the constric-
tion that Gulley feels in his relation to her. Inevitably he
leaves her, although not until they have been together for
nearly five years. But she is not alone for long.

The new focus of her life is Thomas Wilcher. She goes
to his house, Tolbrook, only because she cannot get a
character; the master of Tolbrook is known to have got in
trouble with the police on account of his advances to the
female servants; and Sara has overdrawn her bank account
so heavily that she almost gets sent to prison. Yet within
a month of her going to Tolbrook, she is so well settled
that she is unwilling to go to London to join Gulley when,
finally, he asks her to do so. She has done for Gulley everything of which she is capable. She has been both mistress
and housekeeper, inspiration and servant. But their
relationship came to an impasse. For Sara can only go on
being Sara—managing, tidying, wanting things to be nice,
hoping that Gulley will become a regular husband, that is,
a conventional man. But it is just this that as an artist
Gulley cannot be. At Tolbrook, on the other hand, Sara
can be caretaker of house and master. It is, as she herself
comes to realize, her rôle. She is shocked by the bitterness

of the Felbys, Wilcher's butler and housekeeper from London, into gratitude that she is not mistress of a house, but cook. "Then it came back to me about what poor Jimson had said about my true home being in the kitchen and that I was a born servant in my soul, and my heart gave a turnover and I felt the true joy of my life as clear and strong as if the big round clock over the chimney mouth was ticking inside me."

Wilcher needs the permanence of a geographical centre. Sara does not. When she is moved from Tolbrook to Wilcher's town house she is indeed heartbroken, at first; for she has grown attached to Tolbrook and she finds Craven Gardens to be a prison. "Now why I did not give notice, I don't know, for I certainly meant to, or get my lot bettered. But I think it was only my rolling way." She is partly right, but also partly wrong. For though Craven Gardens strikes her as being "a slice of a house," she cannot resist making even this into a nest. Without turning a hair, Sara becomes a part of London life; she is even glad of "the peace and quiet of the town without hens and calves waking you up at four in the morning." She likes the Round Pond in Kensington Gardens, even to the sight of an old man breathlessly chasing after a toy sailboat. That is, because Sara rejoices in life, she rejoices that others rejoice. She is herself life delighting in life. She is free.

Sara talks to Wilcher not of practicalities—such as money and his having been summoned for indecent exposure—but of books and God and the evening sky. "It was then," she recollects, "I really got to know the master and his true religious heart. For true religion is in the heart or it is nowhere." And he for his part reminds her that she is a religious woman. 'You believe that we have souls to be saved or ruined and so do I. But you have kept your soul alive and I have nearly smothered mine under law papers and estate business and the cares of the world. Under talk too, for I talk too much about religion and forget that it is not a matter of words, but faith and works and vision.' For Sara is not, and her readers perceive the fact, a woman of words; one of the excellences of her book is that it is written in a style so plain as to make us believe in Sara's inarticulateness, even as we read what purport to be her words. As Wilcher sees, Sara's faith is admirably simple and admirably strong; her works are unending, for she has a vision of herself as housekeeper, as servant; she has the energy and the will to translate her vision into action.

But she goes too far. She becomes a thief—not of course mischievously but because, having met Gulley at a funeral, she became a part of his life again. This involved expense, and she had to steal from Wilcher in order to provide this care. And on the day before her intended marriage to Wilcher, Sara is caught. She is accused of robbery. Characteristically Sara reflects, "I knew I was a guilty woman. I felt the ghost of myself, just floating along in the draft from the stove to the sink and back again. I was not even afraid or unhappy. I was only surprised at myself and my devastations." That is, for Sara, as she sees herself, to live is to sin, and to sin is to suffer punishment. "The everlasting enterprise which was her undoing was also her salvation," Cary says in "The Way a Novel gets Written." "As for the moral and aesthetic revolutions which had been tearing other people's worlds to pieces during her whole life, she was scarcely aware of them. Her morals were the elementary morals of a primitive woman, of nature herself, which do not change; and she was supremely indifferent to politics, religion, economics. She was a female artist who was always composing the same work on the same style, but it is a style which does not go out of fashion."

To be a Pilgrim takes up, in time, where *Herself Surprised* leaves off. But reading the one immediately after the other is a shock. For, and this is Cary's intention, we are in a different world, the subjective world of Thomas Wilcher; and from the very first page of *To be a Pilgrim* the reader is forced to look back at Sara, to appraise her and her view of the world once more. Sara's world is narrow; it is a world in which all women are judged against a standard of kitchenness and every man is regarded as a "poor little manny," that is, as an over-grown boy who must be domesticated. Sara is surprised at herself because she is unreflective; there is never an accretion of self-knowledge that can enable her to see into her own heart. Her talent is for living, not thinking; and she cannot think. For though she feels remorse or sorrow or sadness for a little while, the dynamics of her soul propel her into new experiences in which the past is forgotten. And actually *Herself Surprised*, with its patina of regret (Sara means what she says when she is regretful, but she does not feel it, and feelings are all in all with Sara), is a never-elaborate rationale of her life, an apology. For she feels, that is, she knows, her way of life to be self-justifying because abundantly female—generous, mothering, protecting, sexually invigorating and completing.

Thomas Wilcher is a more complex human being, and it follows that his book must have a more complex structure. Sara, in telling about herself, moves straight through her life and with few exceptions observes chronological order. Decades are dismissed in a sentence or two, for during periods of years at a time "nothing happens." She will tell

us the beginnings and endings of her relationships with
Matt, Gulley and Wilcher; but much of the middle is
omitted because then the nest is built and functions
normally. It is only when the nest is threatened or
destroyed that life is recordable.

Thomas Wilcher is a retired lawyer of seventy-one with
a bad heart. To himself he is no "poor little manny," but
a religious man with a sense of history. He undertakes a
"journal" not in order to justify himself to the world,
which is Sara's motive in *Herself Surprised*, but to explain
himself to himself. He perceives the nature of his tragedy,
that of a man attached to the past who must watch the past
being destroyed, but in his feelings he is the prisoner of
his own rôle in life. If the kitchen is the symbol of Sara's
life, Tolbrook is the symbol of Wilcher's. It is his joy as
it is his prison. It stands both for what Wilcher has done
in his life and for what he has failed to do. Tolbrook now,
like Wilcher himself, has gone to seed; but like Wilcher's
own pilgrim soul its beauty is both wild and dignified.
Nevertheless, he does not want to return to Tolbrook;
he wishes to remain near Sara. All the rest of his family
disapprove, and their wish prevails. But "when we were
in sight of the old house, so hated and so loved, I found
myself laughing." To revisit Tolbrook is not only to recall
the past but to sort it out, to make it make sense.

Everything at Tolbrook, every room, every piece of
furniture, every view from the window brings to Wilcher's
mind a memory of his boyhood. The transitions here, and
throughout the book, from past to present are handled
with such directness as to amount to a technical innovation
of some consequence. Is Wilcher mad? His niece Blanche
thinks so and would have him certified. The other niece,
Ann, from Wilcher's reports, seems to be uncertain

whether her uncle is in his right mind or not. In fact, the delicately handled confusion, and perhaps above all the slyness of Wilcher, are such as to make the reader know of his penchant to wander. But to call Wilcher mad is to suppose Blanche to be sane—that is, it begs the question. What is interesting about Wilcher is not the question of his certifiability but the central and perfectly lucid conflict in his nature.

Wilcher recalls his father and the way he handled the family. The elder Wilcher saw things plain. He was a simple man, an ex-cavalry officer, a man of rules. "His idea of religion was that of Confucius, rules of conduct, carefully taught and justly administered." From the whippings that their father occasionally gave them the children had the refuge of their mother's sitting room, which was always reassuringly peaceful.

Against this self-contained, conservative world is set the present, the creative and therefore destructive younger generation of his niece Ann, a doctor of the newest school, and his nephew Robert, a farmer with new ideas. Jaffery, Wilcher's estate agent, a man whom he hates for having a contempt of the past—Jaffery proposes that Wilcher advance some money so that Robert can make improvements. Wilcher resists, but perceives, and thus allows the reader to perceive, Jaffery's exasperation with a difficult old man. Wilcher shouts at Jaffery and has a heart attack which keeps him in bed for two days. Here he thinks of Tolbrook and hates it. "To love anything or anybody is dangerous; but especially to love things." And for the time being he longs to move on, "even for an asylum."

He longs for Sara because her own pilgrim soul, her living instinctive faith, "saved my soul alive" when "my faith was as dead as my heart; and what is faith but the belief that in life there is something worth doing, and the feeling of it." Sara will be out of prison in a year; he looks forward to that as the time of his salvation. 'With you,' he writes to her, or thinks he writes, 'I can make a new life, and unless life be made, it is no life. For we are the children of creation, and we cannot escape our fate, which is to live in creating and re-creating. We must renew ourselves or die. . . . We are the pilgrims who must sleep every night beneath a new sky, for either we go forward to the new camp, or the whirling earth carries us backward to the one behind.' But the reader already knows that an escape to Sara, even if it can be achieved, cannot settle the conflict in Wilcher's soul.

For in a sense it was settled long ago—in the sense that from a young man Wilcher made the terms of his own entrapment. To live his father's life was of course impossible even in Wilcher's own youth; but equally impossible were the courses pursued by his brothers and sister. Wilcher's faith was too deep to be abandoned for the desperate nihilism of his elder brother Edward, who gave up a promising career in the government; his faith was too complex to reduce itself to the notion of duty by which his soldier brother Bill lived; his temperament was too conservative to respond more than sporadically to the enthusiasm of his sister Lucy, who eloped with a Benjamite preacher. But by this last course he was specially tempted. "How did Lucy know at twenty-one, even in her whims, what I don't know till now from all my books, that the way to a satisfying life, a good life, is through an act of faith and courage?" Not happiness and comfort but adventure is the protestant secret of a protestant pilgrimage. At that time in Lucy's life, Wilcher pursued her to a shockingly ugly and dirty industrial town. He had gone to bring her back. He found her scrubbing floors; and though she admitted that she had no rest, she said, 'I have the joy of the Lord.' It was a crisis in Wilcher's life, for he understood the force of this assertion. He felt, though he was not by any means an unsophisticated man, the magnet strength of the Benjamite faith, even though he observed at the same time the squalor, the stupidity, even the hypocrisy of Lucy's husband's life. "It was as though a dark wave had stretched itself before me in a bright and calm night, inviting me to approach." Though he fled Lucy, and though he told Edward a scornful story of the Benjamites, his scorn was wrought out of his own anguish, his impulse to succumb.

As a man in his eighth decade he draws up a balance sheet of his life, in which he very accurately diagnoses his own failure; and his conclusion is that "though I am not a good man, I need not fall into the vanity of supposing myself a monster." This he says not in extenuation of his failure but to prevent "the luxury of those romantic ecstasies by which an Alfred de Musset makes of his common and vulgar sins a special glory." He thinks of Sara, "and the very thought of Sara, as usual brings me peace. For that was Sara's quality. Not the passion of Lucy which transported the soul out of darkness; but the tranquil light, like that of an English morning, which disperses shadows out of all corners."

By the end of the book, Wilcher has come to a new point of resolution. "I say no longer 'Change must come, and this change, so bitter to me, is a necessary ransom for what I keep.' I have surrendered because I cannot fight and now it seems to me that not change but life has lifted me and carried me forward on the stream." Not change but life—a fact admitted to consciousness only when Wilcher is upon the point of death. It is a fact which Sara Monday has always known, by instinct; a fact which Gulley Jimson discovered as a young man. But neither of them has a sense of the past, and it is just this, the sense of historical Englishness, which makes *To be a Pilgrim* excellent in a way different from the excellence of *Herself Surprised* and *The Horse's Mouth*. To Sara the past has no existence, not even her own—she forgets it. To Gulley history is bunk—unforgettable indeed, but imprisoning to the degree that it is remembered, for history is an abstraction and Wilcher himself is to Gulley—as he says in *The Horse's Mouth*, summoning Blake—"abstract philosophy warring in enmity against imagination." Yet Gulley, like Blake, for all his insistence that the now and the particular are what count, knows that imagination must find a form; and it is just there, but only there, that he and Wilcher can meet. Fundamentally the two men are opposites; they are not parallel lines which never intersect.

Gulley Jimson is writing for reasons in perfect harmony with his nature. He is writing because he cannot paint. For, although the reader does not learn this fact until near the end of the book, Gulley is lying in the hospital having suffered a stroke. So he is "dictating this memoir, to my honorary secretary, who has got the afternoon off from the cheese counter." *Herself Surprised* is at once a confession and a rationale; Wilcher's book is an inquiry into the nature of a pilgrimage; *The Horse's Mouth* is neither of these things: it is itself a vast painting, an epic "which won't be published anyhow." It is a portrait of an artist undertaken neither to teach nor to explain, but impulsively, to create.

It says something, just because it is something. The very title suggests the paramount importance of the artist in the world; the artist gets his truth straight from the horse's mouth; he is an interpreter of the vision of God to man. Gulley, the artist, is doomed to misconstruction, to neglect, to persecution, to actual prison as well as to the prison of his isolation from his fellow mortals. 'The old horse doesn't speak only horse,' he says to his friend Nosy, 'and I can't speak only Greenbank.' In the face of this incomprehension and this hostility Gulley must go on creating, for he is a true artist, who can be destroyed but never defeated. And his laughter is a desperate remedy against the world which continually threatens to paralyse him.

Gulley at the beginning of his book has just been freed from prison, and as he walks along the Thames in the misty sunlight he is put in mind—by way of seeing, for the visual, naturally enough, is Gulley's route to both discovery and recovery—of the first lines of Blake's *Europe*. It is Gulley's motive, as it is his style, to "see small portions of the eternal world." Sara and Wilcher, on the other hand, are blind. Sara lives by her instinct, from day to day. Her intimations of immortality are intimations only. And Wilcher is the prisoner of memory. But Gulley's world, even his own private world, is one of eternal creation and recreation.

The world of creation is a world of injustice, and injustice is a major theme of *The Horse's Mouth*. Gulley himself is a painter inhibited from painting because he has no paints—he must "borrow" them. Coker, the barmaid at the Eagle, is physically repulsive and her young man Willy has just gone off with another girl. Captain Smith, a patron of the Eagle, has a daughter of twenty who is already going deaf. Gulley, of course, thinks of this world in visual terms. "I saw all the deaf, blind, ugly, cross-eyed, limp-legged, bulge-headed, bald and crooked girls in the world, sitting on little white mountains and weeping tears like sleet. There was a great clock ticking, and every time it ticked the tears all fell together with a noise like broken glass tinkling in a plate. And the ground trembled like a sleeping dog in front of the parlour fire when the bell tolls for a funeral."

But it is also a world of unsolicited loyalties, of profound and disinterested affections—even in the Strand-on-the-Green which Cary calls Greenbank. Nosy Barbon, a grubby youth in love with art, is determined to protect Gulley. He brings him coffee and buns from the stall, and will not go away even when Gulley impatiently dismisses him. Another friend is Walter Ollier, the postman, who often gives Gulley coffee in the morning and who attends meetings at the house of Godfrey Plant the cobbler. "I liked Plant's club because Plant had beer for his friends." Even Coker is a friend, and her fierceness to Gulley stems not at all from dislike or from the fact that he has not repaid his debt to her, but from an inarticulable despair at the knowledge of another fellow-sufferer from injustice.

Sympathy and affection bring people together: there is communication on that level: Coker and Gulley are together in their sympathies. But for the rest, for comprehension between human beings, it does not exist. This fact is illustrated when Gulley is visited in his boathouse by Godfrey Plant and "two other preachers." It is not a successful visit, for "the trouble is that though all good Protestant preachers round Greenbank including anarchists and anti-God blackboys love beauty, they all hate pictures, real pictures." Plantie is sympathetic. That is, he has brought the preachers there and wants the visit to be a success. He explains the paintings clearly but uncomprehendingly. Gulley is cast down—"the more he tried, the worse I felt." And instead of attending to the philistine remarks of the preachers, Gulley thinks of "The Mental Traveller," which for twenty pages he cites, reflects on and interprets. Of all the Blake to be found in *The Horse's Mouth*, this is surely the most important. Cary himself regarded it as central both to an understanding of Blake and to an understanding of *The Horse's Mouth*.

"The Mental Traveller" is open to several interpretations. Cary himself suggested that the poem may be read in several different ways, but he did not offer this suggestion as a complaint against it. Gulley Jimson, however, is unvexed. He interprets the poem as recording the cycle of artistic creation. Indeed, he puts Plantie and the preachers into the poem. Plantie himself is one of those who "nails him down upon a rock, Catches his shrieks in cups of gold." Gulley's gloss here, and it is typical, is: "Which means that some old woman of a blue nose nails your work of imagination to the rock of law, and why and what; and submits him to a logical analysis."

Gulley's term for his present feeling is grief; Sara's term in her own book, for she does not understand Gulley as he understands himself, is stuck. And on the occasions when Sara uses this word of him, he hits her. Walking in the open air on Greenbank "to get room for my grief," Gulley thinks of Sara as the female and thus as both the completing and the constricting principle in his life. He recollects the story of his relationship with her against the remembered lines of "The Mental Traveller," and he exposes with perfect clarity the nature of Sara as he sees her.

> *She binds iron thorns around his head,*
> *She pierces both his hands and feet,*
> *She cuts his heart out at his side*
> *To make it feel both cold and heat.*

JOYCE CARY

Her fingers number every nerve
Just as a miser counts his gold;
She lives upon his shrieks and cries,
And she grows young as he grows old.

"She," as he recollects these lines, is explicitly Sara; and Sara is the feminine principle. She is thus material as against Gulley's spirit. In order for the spirit to be expressed, material is required—yet unless, until, the spirit dominates, it will be choked. Thus Gulley, like Blake, draws close parallels between sexuality and artistic creation.

Then he rends up his manacles
And binds her down for his delight.
He plants himself in all her nerves,
Just as a husbandman his mould;
And she becomes his dwelling place
And garden fruitful seventy fold.

Or, as the desperate Gulley puts it, but still with relish: "Materiality, that is, Sara, the old female nature, having attempted to button up the prophetic spirit, that is to say, Gulley Jimson, in her placket-hole, got a bonk on the conk, and was reduced to her proper status, as spiritual fodder. But what fodder. What a time that was."

In an attempt to protect Gulley from the police—he has been uttering menaces against his patron Hickson—Franklin and Ollier take him down to the river, where they put him in charge of a boatman, Bert Swope, and a dwarf named Harry. These men do not understand Gulley as an artist, but they sympathize with him as a human being. But to Gulley this is, at the moment, little consolation, for he is reflecting on the agonies of an artist's life.

He recollects that he never intended to become an artist; indeed he had determined never to become one. Having seen his father's work become outmoded, having seen him, "a little grey-bearded old man, crying in the garden," because his style went out of fashion, Gulley started respectably as a business man in the City. "But one day when I was sitting in our London office on Bankside, I dropped a blot on an envelope; and having nothing to do just then, I pushed it about with my pen to try to make it look more like a face." That was the beginning, the disease from which Gulley has never recovered. He rehearses the stages of his life as an artist, his continual efforts to catch, in "Mental Traveller" terms, the maiden. "The job," Gulley says, "is always to get hold of the form you need." But the form is elusive; for the intuition changes, develops; the eyes see things ever differently if the artist is not to become fatally imprisoned by one form of expression, one style—as did Gulley's father. Now Gulley, an old man in despair, reflects, "I've lost sight of the maiden altogether. I wander weeping far away, until some other take me in. The police. It's quite time. I'm getting too old for this rackety life."

On this evening of despair, Gulley with the others meets Plantie, who is full of excitement that Professor Ponting, from America, is going to address his meeting. The subject is to be "Religion and Humanity." It is a grubby meeting of grubby life-defeated people in a bed-sitting room behind Plantie's shop. Sara appears, and she and Gulley converse in the scullery. She has sought him out. She is immensely depressed, for—as she tells Gulley—she hates feeling old. But the fact is, she is not well and she is afraid that Fred, the man with whom she is now living, will put her in hospital. 'Oh Gulley,' she says, 'if I could trust you to keep me out of those hospitals and infirmaries, I believe I'd go off with you.' In the meantime, and contrapuntal to the conversation between Gulley and Sara, Professor Ponting is delivering his talk; the theme is "the boundless possibilities of human happiness." It is a touching juxtaposition here, of Sara's old woman talk and the skate-faced Ponting's rolling platitudes: a tragicomic incident altogether, ending roisteringly in Gulley's and Sara's drinking too much and trying to make love in the scullery. The closing song they sing, "Jerusalem," is an ironical comment on the meeting. For it is, in Blakean terms, artists who build Jerusalem, not such people as the skate and his audience. But there is more than irony here, more than coarsely mirthful contrast: "there is," Professor Milton Percival points out, "pathos in the supposition, on the part of these people, that they *are* building it. And perhaps they are, in their bewildered way."

This episode can be seen in expanded, more explicit form in the discarded section of *The Horse's Mouth* called "The Old Strife at Plant's," which was published in *Harper's* magazine several years ago, and also privately printed in Oxford in 1956. And it is not difficult to see why the discarded chapter was in fact discarded. For though it is brilliant, in some ways more brilliant than what appears in the novel itself, it is not germane. It does not fit into the economy of the novel. In the novel the woman is Sara, and when Gulley at the end of the evening puts her on the last bus home, he realizes what this encounter has meant to him. "I could see the woman inside: the real Sara that had made me mad, especially with the brush . . . the everlasting Eve, but all alive-oh." As she excites him she inspires him, and at a time when he stands greatly in need of inspiration.

But the discarded section, besides being several times as

long as what was finally incorporated into the novel, contains, instead of Sara, another ancient woman, Sukey, whom the reader never meets elsewhere. Furthermore, there is an extra dimension in the discarded chapter. While Sukey is retailing a saga of her life with Bill and Grandma and fourteen children, Gulley is making scratches on a beer bottle. The skate is meanwhile preaching platitudes much as he does in the finished version. But in the finished version Gulley and Sara really converse—they talk to one another; whereas in the discarded section Sukey's tale is a background to the inspiration which Gulley has, or thinks he has, at Plant's. That is, the discarded section is too schematic. Still, Sukey is an admirable creation, a nakeder, cruder, simpler Sara. At the end, the vision at the bus is more explicit than it is in the finished version. 'My beauty,' I cried, 'my fulfillment, my life, I have you at last, and you shall after have me, in happiness ever after—after? AFTER! HI, STOP HER, SOMEONE. STOP DARLING, DAMN YOU DARLING.'

Gulley is therefore wrong to suppose himself too old. He remains alive just because he can see, because he can "face the world down," just because—as Sara also says—"he can be all serene." It is those who are blind who suffer most keenly. Nor will Gulley, like Housman, "endure a while and see injustice done;" he will never surrender to injustice. This point is illustrated by his encounter with Plant some months after the meeting described above. Gulley has spent the winter in prison for theft and destruction of Hickson's property. When he looks for Plant he finds him gone. The cobbler got blood poisoning after running a needle into his right hand; he has had to have it amputated; too proud to accept any help, he has gone to a doss-house called Elsinore. There Gulley finds him among a scramble of sixpenny customers, fighting with one another for the use of the three frying pans in the kitchen. In the ugly mélange sits Plant, utterly defeated. He holds up his stump to Gulley in confusion. 'It means something,' he says. 'It can't be wasted. It's a revelation. It makes me feel like I never knew anything before.' And when Plant repeatedly fails to capture one of the frying pans, when at last he is flung contemptuously into a corner by a young man, he is reduced to tears. "But," Gulley reflects, "it's natural. He's got a sense of justice. Poor old chap. And he can't get over it—not at his age."

Gulley himself, well schooled in injustice, knows better than to expect justice, but his knowledge is not always or altogether consoling. He recollects with bitterness his sister Jenny running off at the age of eighteen with a married man of thirty-five. In a year she was transformed from a fresh-faced girl to skin and bones. 'It made me swear, Mr Plant. But I was young then. Young and innocent. I didn't make allowances for other people doing what they liked, as well as myself.' Indeed, the story of Jenny is told intermittently throughout *The Horse's Mouth*—haunting Gulley because it was so terribly unjust; for Jenny, having made every sacrifice to her husband, had to endure his leaving her. But she did not endure it for long. She took her own life.

The adventure with Sir William and Lady Beeder provides a variation on the theme—but it is a necessary variation, because it takes Gulley out of Greenbank for a considerable period of time, into a larger or at least a different world. He is delighted with these rich and stupid patrons of the arts. "What I like about the rich is the freedom and friendliness. Christian atmosphere. Liberty Hall. Everything shared because there is too much. All forgiveness because it's no trouble." And there are, I suppose, few funnier episodes in all fiction than the account of Gulley's afternoon and evening with the Beeders. They are perfect material for Gulley to work on. Lady Beeder paints—a little, and when an example of her work is shown to Gulley, he is charming about it, for a moment; then his charm becomes gay malice. He says, 'All this amateur stuff is like farting Annie Laurie through a keyhole. It may be clever but is it worth the trouble? What I say is, why not do some real work, your ladyship. Use your loaf, I mean your brain. Do some thinking. Sit down and ask yourself what's it all about.'

During dinner—for Gulley remains until the Beeders must ask him to dine—he drinks too much and in his intoxication he is transported to the land of Beulah. Lady Beeder is so beautiful, so charming, so respectful and friendly; so silly, shallow and uncomprehending. 'But do you think,' she asks Gulley, 'that mad people really suffer?' And it is precisely Beulah that describes Gulley's state—Blake's Beulah, which, as Professor Percival says, is "a land where the doubting masculine mind is put to sleep and enclosed in a protective space by the daughters of Beulah (the benevolent emotions). The daughters urge the sleeper to take it easy for a time and not think (dispute), lest it think itself into a fall."

When the Beeders go off to America, Gulley takes possession of their flat. He begins quietly enough: he removes the paintings in order to find the right wall on which to paint the Raising of Lazarus. He then sketches feet on the wall—big feet, little feet, young feet, old feet, Lord's feet. Next he decides to take an advance on this masterpiece to be, and so he pawns Lady Beeder's teapot and some spoons. But this is only the beginning. He pawns more and more of the furnishings, and gets in all the equipment he needs to undertake his painting. He hires models. He even allows the friend of a friend to come in and begin work on a war memorial. This man is a sculptor named Abel, whose determination and enthusiasm quite equal Gulley's. After a very few weeks, Gulley and Abel have not only caused to be removed everything of value in the flat—even the lavatory chain—but they have ruined the floors and walls.

When at last the Beeders return, Gulley flees raging against the world's injustice—forgetting because as artist he must forget how unjust he himself has been; and after an entr'acte the last movement of the novel begins. The subject of this movement is the Creation, as it is the subject of Gulley's last painting. He has a sense that he is working against the tolling bell of his own mortality; he has a sense of his agedness. Besides, he has murdered Sara, not maliciously but because she interfered with his effort to take a painting from her flat, with which he could buy paints and equipment for the Creation.

Getting to work on a huge wall in a dilapidated building —a ruined chapel, in fact—in an alley off Horsemonger's Yard, Gulley is so excited that he says, 'it will probably bring up an earthquake, or a European war and wreck half the town.' This in answer to Nosy, who wants to have the roof propped up before Gulley begins. He ignores a representative of the council who serves notice on Gulley to get out because the building is unsafe. But the work proceeds. Gulley stays.

When the activity is at its height, Sir William Beeder and other men of influence visit the chapel. But they have come, as he discovers, not to admire his wall, and not to do anything about preventing it from being knocked down, but to ask him to accept a commission to paint a portrait of a general. From the moment this revelation is made to Gulley he forgets, or at least omits to regard, what the deputation says. And a little later from Nosy, who has set spies on the deputation, he learns that even these important patrons have been plotting against him; for, wanting him to paint portraits rather than walls, they support the efforts of the borough council to get him out of the ruined chapel. "Now this was the very voice of the original serpent. It is only too easy to believe that something is going on behind one's back; because, of course, it always is."

For consolation Gulley goes to the Feathers, "and seeing Alfred's old white cat coming out at the door, I caught her and carried her in. I wanted some kindness. And no one is more kind than a cat. Her own kind." For Gulley, this cat, a deaf and castrated animal named Snow, provides a focus and a solace. Snow is alone. "She didn't look anywhere but she never touched a puddle. Keeping herself to herself. Tiger, tiger, burning bright." Even when Alfred the barman tickles her, she pays no attention—just as Gulley wishes he could ignore the Feathers patron who berates him for painting muck—'we *know* it's muck'—on the chapel wall in Horsemonger's Yard. 'Ya. You can talk. But you've done for yourself. They'll take your dirty picture away and burn it.' Snow is beyond such ranting, and Gulley feels a flow of sympathy for her. Gulley, equally isolated but more involved, connects the destruction of his wall with the destruction of the world: art and war.

But it is not only Snow who is alone in this room. Coker is also living in a world by herself. As the Feathers patrons talk, she looks absent-mindedly at Gulley's empty can and forgets to fill it. Her mind is on her own creation. "Her

JOYCE CARY

mind was in the snug, trying to make sure the basket was still asleep; or examining his features to see if he was likely to be a Prime Minister." Even a young soldier in the bar is self-contained, jealous of his own privacy: when someone asks him what his job is, he replies, 'Here, you want to know a lot, don't you? Perhaps you'd like to see my birthmark.' And he walks indignantly out of the pub. The patrons of the Feathers are indeed like Snow. As Alfred says of her, 'You can't tell what's going on inside her.' Gulley's characteristic reply is, 'Probably cat . . . or that's what I should think.'

At last Gulley returns to Horsemonger's Yard and ascends his wall. "Till I was swinging about in the air, thirty feet from the ground, like an angel." He is so grief-struck at Sara's death that he can hardly paint. Nevertheless, in the combined fevers of sorrow, drunkenness, anxiety and desperation, he paints. Sara returns to him in his delirium and urges him to take care of himself, to go to bed. And in the course of this imaginary conversation, Gulley puts into Sara's mouth the quintessential truth about their relationship. 'Oh you properly doted on me, Gulley, didn't you?' 'Sometimes, Sall.' 'And that's why you hit me on the nose, didn't you, Gulley? Because you didn't like me being on your mind. You didn't like not to be free, did you?' And, as he has always done before, he now dismisses Sara—sorrowfully but with finality. For he must be free. He must paint.

He dozes till daylight, when he is awakened by a police-man who has come not to arrest him for the murder of Sara—she, loyal to the end, has described her assailant as a tall, red-haired man with a foreign accent—but to assist in the eviction of Gulley from the chapel. The demolition has begun. Gulley ignores the noise, the dust, the voices

136

below him. He keeps on painting, keeps on creating, keeps on keeping on. Until at last "the whale smiled. Her eyes grew bigger and brighter and she bent slowly forward as if she wanted to kiss me. . . . And all at once the smile broke in half, the eyes crumpled, and the whole wall fell slowly away from my brush. . . ." At last, after the dust has cleared somewhat, and after he has seen "about ten thousand angels in caps, helmets, bowlers, and even one top hat" laughing at him—all classes of respectable society laughing at Gulley Jimson the artist—at last, alone on the swing high above the sea of faces, Gulley is finished. He is flung down from his cradle, paralysed by a stroke, and hauled away in a police ambulance. When Nosy in tears complains of the injustice, Gulley replies, 'Get rid of that sense of justice, Nosy, or you'll feel sorry for yourself, and then you'll be dead—blind and deaf and rotten.' Gulley's prescription is Blake's prescription. "Go love," Blake writes in the *Gnomic Verses*, and Gulley quotes the phrase now, "without the help of anything on earth." In this wisdom, in the splendour of his isolation, in the amplitude of his own created world, Gulley can even now face the other worlds down. He can, even mortally ill, keep on keeping on. He can be all serene. For though all men are free, the artist is the most free. Liberated by a special grace, Gulley can tell the nun in the police ambulance that laughter is the same thing as prayer.

3 *The Political Trilogy*

The *raisons d'être* of all the volumes of the political trilogy are especially well established. Nina in *Prisoner of Grace* is justifying her rôle by answering "revelations" that have been made about Nimmo and herself—the penny-press sensationalism which can pass for history only because it is faithful to the facts, the debunking biography which looks for clay feet, and the hagiography which exalts Nimmo at the expense of his wife and friends. Nina's brand of revision also involves distortion: so there are several possible versions set out in *Prisoner of Grace* alone. But there is yet another in *Except the Lord*, which is also an apology, this time by Nimmo, who discovers in the evangelical background of his poverty-stricken family the source and cast of his life, both as a man and as a politician. It is a moving self-portrait, but it stops when Nimmo is on the threshold of his political career, so that the reader is forced by the act of retrospection to understand the sources of the man's motive; and, implicitly, asked to forgive. The narrator of *Not Honour More* is about to be hanged—or, as he says, hung—for the murder of his wife, or else to be certified criminally insane; and he must justify his action to himself and to a world that he wishes could be run along lines of decency and justice—meaning by these words soldier-decency and soldier-justice. Latter's version of Nimmo is a bitter portrait of a supple politician drawn by an inflexible soldier who is corroded by the acids of jealousy.

Nina's book has the flavour of retrospect not simply because it surveys her past, but because it does so from the vantage point of what is formally, though not actually, a new phase in her life. The book centres on her relationship to Chester Nimmo, as his wife, as a prisoner of grace. But she tells her story when she has become Mrs James Latter. It is true to say that she has always been in spirit Latter's wife—her children are his children; but it is equally true that she can never escape from her imprisonment by Nimmo. At the end of the book he has come to her house and made his claims, which she cannot refuse. So the formal device of the book clearly emphasizes the personal boundaries of Nina's life. She stands between the two men, sometimes as mediator, but always as comforter to them both.

Nina ascribes her acquiescence to Chester's proposal of marriage—she is seventeen and pregnant by Jim Latter—to a tendency to dawdle. "I had begun to suspect that I could reconcile myself to anything." This is a key to her character, one that fits the lock to so many puzzles in her life. But Nina, betrayed as always by her curiously involuted style, is less than fair to herself. She is not, as she thinks, adrift on a wave over which she has no control. She is loyal. Even before the crisis when she almost left Chester, she was loyal. At the time of the Boer War, Chester was a pacifist. At one political meeting he called the soldiers fighting the war, murderers and cowards. When he repeated this charge elsewhere, a bad riot ensued. Both he and Nina were subjected to rough treatment. But these incidents brought Chester into national prominence and Nina was hailed as a heroine of the cause. She did indeed work hard for Chester in this period, not because she had been converted to his kind of radicalism, but because "I was afraid of what would happen to me, if I came to hate Chester. My devotion, in fact, was like those embraces and kisses I had used to give Jim as a child when I met him at the station and remembered all our fearful quarrels. They were a kind of incantation to make me love."

But the conclusive test occurs after the Boer War, when Jim returns to England. Almost as soon as he and Nina meet, Jim makes love to her, and they agree to go away together. 'We have got,' Jim says, 'to be free.' The next morning Nina leaves Chester, as she thinks for ever. But he follows her to the railway station. And here occurs the crucial scene in the book. Chester's persuasion is considerate, loving and finally irresistible.

'So you want to go to Jim?'

'Don't you see I must go.'

'I was putting the emphasis on "want." Do you *want* to go to Jim or only to escape from me?'

'Please, Chester, don't cross-examine me—it's too late; it really is too late. You mustn't stop me now; you can't.' He brings up an old argument that in marrying him she married out of her class. But this infuriates and confuses Nina. He also brings up the subject of religion. 'I really think, Nina, that our life together has had God's blessing upon it, and you might blame yourself if you broke it up.' Then, after further argument, Chester simply gets up and leaves.

When the train arrives, Nina starts for it. "But when I reached the door my feet stopped and turned me aside. I simply could not go out, and neither could I make up my mind to stay. I went a step to one side, and then came back to the door, but absolutely stuck there. I seemed to have no will to do anything, or rather I had two wills which were fighting inside me and tearing me apart. I can never forget the agony of that time, which must actually have lasted three or four minutes before the train went out. And really I think it was a kind of relief to me when at last it did so, for it made a decision for me."

A good deal later in the book, when she knows him much better, Nina writes that Chester has a number of strong defences, "but if you did break through, you found inside always at least some part of the original Chester." For Chester at last "had recollected that Jim and Tom were individual persons." This is, I think, one more crucial revelation on Nina's part; it goes a long way toward suggesting the terms of her voluntary imprisonment by grace. The "original Chester," the real man, is what binds Nina in thrall of the allegiance of a lifetime. This thralldom even makes it possible for Nina to endure, though she does so with anguish, the ruin of her son Tom, who is gifted and sensitive, and who adores Chester, yet is overwhelmed by him. "Chester was like a drug to him . . . and too much of it produced a reaction."

The book, in justifying Chester, justifies by explaining the necessity of political manœuvre. Having been privately warned of a possible scandal concerning his financial holdings, Chester sells some shares quickly and is able to make a satisfying—though not fully candid—explanation in the House. But to tell the whole story "would have been *quite* misleading. . . . It might have produced a *great injustice*, that is, the ruin of Chester's career." Nina defends him strongly. "Chester was quite right, therefore, to arrange his statement so that people were persuaded to believe that he was really innocent, because he *was innocent*. And it was true to say that he had no warning which enabled him to 'cover up,' because he had nothing to 'cover up' in the sense in which his enemies used the word."

This impassioned defence by Nina is also part of the book's defence of the man. Nina is described by Cary himself in the Carfax preface as a credible witness. "I'd like to know," says Nina, and here she is, it seems to me, echoing Cary's own sentiments, "what would happen if nobody tried to manage people, if mothers always told the facts to children (saying to the stupid ones that they were stupid) and never took any consideration for their nerves and their fits of temper and fights and silliness." Indeed,

JOYCE CARY

Cary has used almost these very words elsewhere, and in his own person, to define "politics" in its widest sense. "And what I am trying to do in this book," Nina says, and again I think she is echoing Cary, "is not to make out that Chester was a saint (which would be stupid, after all the books and articles about him) but to show that he was, in spite of the books, a 'good man'—I mean (and it is saying more than could be said of most people) as good as he could be in his special circumstances and better than many were in much easier ones."

The political trilogy does, it seems to me, turn on this plea, and within it is the structure of the map which Cary is drawing in the political trilogy altogether. In the human drama Chester is in favour of wangling as against shooting; Jim, seeing the world in black-and-white terms, favours shooting to maintain his ideal of justice. And Nina is the mediator, sympathizing with both men, bound to them both. The tension in Cary's novels is always between these two poles, and the positions are not reconcilable. There is no golden mean.

The shock of reading *Except the Lord* after *Prisoner of Grace* derives in part from the fact that the novels of this trilogy are written out of order: in *Prisoner of Grace* Nina meets Chester when he is in his early thirties; *Except the Lord* deals with his childhood and youth, and it provides another kind of justification; it is written by Lord Nimmo himself at the very end of his life. The book, however, stops far short of considering the man at the summit of his powers, perhaps because Chester cannot deal with these years: the irony of *Except the Lord*—unexpressed by Chester—is that for its hero lordship becomes merely an empty symbol of temporal possession.

THE INEVITABLE STYLE

His style is richly evangelical. "Yesterday, an old man nearing my end, I stood by the grave of a noble woman, one of the three noblest I have ever known, my mother, my sister, my wife. If I draw back now the curtain from my family life, sacred to memory, I do so only to honour the dead, and in the conviction that my story throws light upon the crisis that so fearfully shakes our whole civilization."

As Chester recalls his youth, he often shifts to the present tense, a device which in conveying a sense of the immediacy of these events to the reader conveys also the sense of Chester's own intimate relationship to them. "I have been sent to the shop to meet Georgina, because on the Saturday, she will have a heavy bag of groceries and she is just out of bed. Georgina, though so dark and wiry, had lately had influenza, and a touch of pleurisy, and the doctor when he came to see my mother had warned us that the girl was working beyond her strength." Here the juxtaposition of tenses serves the double purpose of suggesting both the vividness of the recollection and the nostalgia which it evokes. Furthermore the book is, throughout, extremely episodic. There are flashes of recollection, in chronological order to be sure, but there is not a usual kind of continuity. No doubt this is intended by the author, who wishes to show, among other things, the urgency Chester feels laid upon himself to explain himself to the world—before it is too late.

Indeed, a sense of doom pervades the whole. This is illustrated when Chester recalls the harvest season during which he and his brother and sister want to go to the Lilmouth Great Fair. To get together enough money is an undertaking of great difficulty. There is a tin miners' strike on, supported financially and spiritually by their father. Before the fair, old Nimmo takes his two sons to a hillside meeting of the striking miners, and it is a meeting which Chester never forgets, for it is a sight of appalling poverty, of men and women and children starved. Old Nimmo wants to urge—though he does not do so directly, and he does not insist—the children's support of the miners in their distress. "Ah, I hear you say, a typical Victorian despotism, a hypocritical theocracy in which children were robbed of all freedom and joy—even of their own earnings—in the name of a Divine Providence that was in fact the whim of the paternal autocrat. Nothing could be more untrue; I doubt if that parent ever existed except for the purposes of professional novelists—a not very reputable tribe, eager, as your friends in America put it, to 'cash in' on the usual reaction of every age against the last."

This paragraph tells implicitly of Chester's own sense of audience as he writes, an old man now regarded as hopelessly out of date. The whole book thus is written for readers whom he knows to be unsympathetic. Having been a great man, swept from popular triumph to popular triumph, having almost succeeded in becoming Prime Minister, he has gone—we know from Nina's story—to defeat in two general elections, and from there to the defeat of a peerage. Death is near. And the style of this book is therefore anxious, patiently impatient, even sometimes bewildered, paranoid.

Toward the end of the book Chester states the circumstances under which he is writing. An old man who has just had a heart attack, he is dictating to her "who has been my wife" in order "to dispel through these memoirs a cloud of misunderstanding which has thrown so black a shade upon my last hours." The reader of *Prisoner of Grace* knows that Chester is in Palm Cottage dictating to a Nina who has become Mrs Latter; and taking bold advantage of her sexually, whenever the two of them are alone together. He is moved to remark on the fundamental nature of women, whose politics are not that of affairs but the politics of home and hearth. In the context of *Except the Lord*, this reflection has a pious ring; but behind this context is that of *Prisoner of Grace*: the reflection is not only pious, it is also, and equally, lascivious.

"The crisis that so fearfully shakes our whole civilization" is, as the reader of *Prisoner of Grace* knows, what Chester has come to feel is the disease of the post-war generation, the departure in the 1920s from the religious principles which have animated Chester's whole life. The book, written by a man who is himself lost, is an indictment of the lost generation. Chester decries the abandonment of the fundamental revelation of Jesus, of a faith in Divine Providence, of the relationship—personal, intimate, Protestant—between man and God. *Except the Lord* sets out to rediscover the roots of Chester's own religion, his orientation to the world. The truly Protestant cast of Chester's mind is revealed again and again in the entire trilogy, not least in his reaction to the Italian churches which he and Nina see when they are on their honeymoon. He does not like them; he finds them, Nina says in *Prisoner of Grace*, "even worse than he had expected." "He meant that they were full of saints and candles. For he had a horror of the Roman religion and said that wherever it had power you found ignorance and oppression and dirt and poverty. I said that perhaps that was because miserable ignorant people needed a nice rich artistic kind of religion, but this also shocked him and he said with his religious voice, 'artistic religion isn't religion at all—how could it be? There is only one true religion—between a man's own soul and his God'."

Chester is the son of an impoverished yeoman who is also a lay preacher; a man farming forty acres in Devonshire. Chester's mother is the daughter of a schoolmaster. Old Nimmo believes in the Second Coming and is a man of great generosity. But one of Chester's earliest recollections is that of his father refusing a man ten shillings for drink. "How cruel," writes Chester, "is that charge of the selfish against the Christian, often poorer than himself, 'You profess Christ, therefore you have no right to refuse me anything.' In fifty years of politics, I have not known worse—it wounds so deep." Whom has Chester himself refused? The reader of *Prisoner of Grace* recalls that Chester has refused to see his patron and old friend, Goold, when the two men are at odds on the issue of pacifism at the outbreak of the First World War; he has often refused to assist Jim Latter in his career, though he has helped him too; he has refused even to help young Tom Nimmo when the boy was threatened with prison. All these refusals he undertook on the summoning up of principle, an exercise which Nina finds to be convenient, self-deceiving. But there can be little doubt that these principles are sincerely, religiously adhered to—or revealed—and it is in the environment of which he now writes that he has learned about God.

Chester calls the Lilmouth Great Fair "central in my history." And the central experience which Chester has is the shock, the exaltation, of the theatre tent. He speaks of the "vehement tremor of that night" when he sees introduced on the platform the actors of the play. He knows that the theatre is forbidden. He knows that it is evil. But he is drawn irresistibly into the tent.

The play is a melodrama of seduction, or rather the rape, of a poor and virtuous village girl by the villainous son of her parents' landlord. "Throughout the play everything possible was done to show the virtue, innocence and helplessness of the poor, and the abandoned cruelty, the heartless self-indulgence of the rich." The play, Chester says, "was decisive in my own life." The reason is that it opens doors to life's possibilities. "I have heard it said that a man's first experience in the theatre opens a new world to him—it would be better to say that it destroys the old one." But what strikes him deeper than the theme of the play, the terrible injustice visited by a "gentleman" upon a helpless girl, what horrifies him most profoundly of all is the "fascinated admiration" which he feels for the villain. "When in his soliloquies at the front of the stage, his eyes, roving over the audience, seemed to meet mine, they sent forth an indescribable thrill—it seemed that something flashed from the very centre of evil into my deepest soul."

Here is the Cary preoccupation with the power of the word for good and for evil: it is the theme of his last novel, *The Captive and the Free*; and the reader must observe that there is no choice between good or evil here: the power of the word is a power for both the one and the other. This is a fact which Chester, by the very importance which he attaches to this recollection, recognizes.

The other decisive event in Chester's life occurs some years later when, now a young man, he becomes a labour agitator and learns the meaning of violence. During a shipping strike, of which Chester is one of the leaders, an offer is made to settle the strike by partly meeting the union's demands. Chester and his cohorts turn this down. Instead they vote for "more activity on picket and more private persuasion," a euphemism for a violence which, in retrospect, Chester regards with horror. The motive,

147

Chester now sees, "in the so-called active policy was violence for the sake of violence, cruelty to make hatred, in short, class war and revolution." When the strike does become more violent, Chester himself witnesses a scene of heart-rending outrage: a house wrecked and the father of a family lying wounded in the street. To his everlasting shame, Chester is cool in the face of this disaster, not heart-rent. He is almost sent to prison; he escapes that fate only by telling lies. And, Chester says, writing now, his whole life might have been ruined had not an accident occurred. He was betrayed by the strike leader himself, who, without consulting Chester, threatened even greater violence; when Chester demurred, he was thrown out, out of the union, out of his lodgings, literally into the street; spiritually sickened by his experience, and soon reduced to physical sickness as well.

To understand all is to forgive all, but to forgive is not to withhold judgment. If the Chester Nimmo of *Prisoner of Grace* is often revoltingly self-deceived, he is equally a pitiable figure by the very profoundness of his self-deception. But even Nina cannot know him as he knows himself. The force and thrust of his own childhood and youth do not impinge upon her judgment as they impinge upon his—and as they impinge upon ours, when we come to know him through his own words in *Except the Lord*. The second volume of the political trilogy widens the boundary of our sympathy for Chester Nimmo, not least because he cannot explain in his own words the events of his political career. But a final judgment is possible only when we see him through the harshly hostile eyes of a madman.

Not Honour More is a soldier's story. Its theme is honour, a soldier's honour, like that of the soldier Lovelace's poem which gives the book its title. Captain James Vandeleur Latter, the narrator of this novel, seeks justice in a world condemned to injustice; he searches for simple truth amidst a thousand indirections. And he is doomed by the very clarity and nobility of his ideas to suffer, indeed to perpetrate, the tragedy which is the murder of his wife.

Temperamentally, Nimmo and Latter are opposites, and to display these two men in conflict is, of course, one of the aims of the political trilogy. "This book," Cary writes in the preface to the German edition of *Not Honour More*, "shows the clash between two fundamental temperaments and these temperaments are permanent in the world. There are always millions of Latters and Nimmos and they will never agree on the ends or even the means of political action." Latter complains that one of his difficulties in writing his book is the almost universal veneration for Nimmo, "built up by the Press as a political racket. Old honest Baldwin with his pipe was nearly as bad. . . . Old Baldwin! As cunning a diddler as any in the book. What do they do it for? Why do they build up these grabbers and fakers into noble souls and heroes of the nation? It's all in the game. Poor devil of a Press artist has to get a job, catch the public eye. Tickle 'em somewhere. Poor devils of the mob want to think they've got a genius to look after 'em, hold off the next slump, keep out the next war. And the politicos make hay between, with their tongues in their cheeks. It's the whole system is wrong. It's the way we've got fixed. By drifting along and not asking where we're getting to." It is here, as often elsewhere, that the reader must be certain that Jim Latter is not Joyce Cary's mouthpiece, but that he is a fanatical man standing condemned on his own testimony which the reader

understands quite clearly between the lines of Jim's own
statement. For instance, Jim alludes to his book, *The Lugas
and British African Policy: The Great Betrayal* (the reader
of *Prisoner of Grace* knows it to have been a failure in every
way), to show his distrust of politicians generally. The
book, written ten years before, excoriated politicians. So,
Jim suggests, there is—or was—nothing personal in his
dislike of Nimmo. "I say my Lugas were better Christians
in every way, and better men than any in Whitehall. They
were truly nature's gentlemen and the finest I ever knew.
But since then entirely ruined and destroyed as a people
by European so-called progress." If there is any doubt at
this point whether such an opinion represents Cary's own
thinking, the reader need only turn to Cary's political
pamphlets, in which he argues eloquently for the bringing
of European civilization to Africa.

When the book opens, Jim Latter is in prison, awaiting,
as he thinks, hanging. The book is a statement hurriedly
made by a condemned man of strong temper. It is "dictated
at high speed for shorthand" to "Policewoman Martin."
The style is the man—blunt, straightforward, harsh,
passionate. The statement begins by recalling an event on
May 1st, 1926, when there is an anonymous telephone call
warning Jim Latter that Chester Nimmo intends to commit
adultery with the woman who is now Mrs James Latter.
The telephone call follows upon anonymous letters
suggesting such a liaison. There is in time and circum-
stance, therefore, a connection to be made between the end
of *Prisoner of Grace* and the beginning of *Not Honour More*.
In the brief interval between, the events foretold in the last
line of *Prisoner of Grace* have taken place: Nina and Chester
have been found out, and Jim has taken her life. If the
public focus of the novel is the 1926 General Strike, the

private focus is the triangular conflict among the three principals—and in the course of the book the two focuses become one. *Not Honour More* establishes, this time catastrophically, the connection between public and private politics.

The book opens with what Jim intends to be an execution. It opens on May Day 1926, when Chester goes to Shagbrook to speak on "God in Politics." Later Jim, returning to Palm Cottage, finds "this old swine over seventy years of age, interfering with my wife." When Jim shoots he is knocked out by Chester's bodyguard. Awakening several hours later, he learns that Chester is not dead. Indeed, Nina urges Jim to tell the reporters and the police that the shooting was accidental. For, she says, Chester is "in his heart . . . a true, good man." Characteristically, Jim is stunned that she should defend this "known crook and wangler;" loving her, he has never understood her: at least he has never understood the aspect of her nature which has made her a prisoner of grace. But Nina brings up "an argument that surprised me even more. 'Oh, Jim, don't you see that if he gets back into office, he'll go away from here and we'll have peace again.'" For in the national crisis which has been developing, there is some considerable possibility that Chester will occupy a commanding position; he may even become Prime Minister.

Jim finds Nina's second reason so extraordinary because he does not understand now, and never has understood, the real complexity of her nature. She has always detested Chester, but she has never been able to escape from her spiritual bondage to him; she has always loved Jim, and now as a wife she adores him: the conflict is irreconcilable; it is therefore not surprising that since she cannot solve it she tries now, as she has tried before, to end it. But Jim, stung by jealousy, cannot believe in her love for him because he cannot comprehend her.

This fact is illustrated by the news handout he gives later in the evening at a public house to which he has escaped from Palm Cottage. In the first place, he accuses Chester of "interfering with my wife." He also makes, in brief compass, his case against Chester as a politician. "My whole case is this, that if a man or country gives up the truth, the absolute truth, they are throwing away the anchor and drifting slowly but surely to destruction. I say nothing can save but truth and the guts to take it. For truth will always prevail." When a reporter tells Jim that the sentence accusing Nimmo of misbehaviour with Mrs Latter is libel and must be omitted, Jim is infuriated. Another reporter asks if he is a Fascist. To this Jim replies: 'That is a foul lie. You know very well I belong to one of the oldest Liberal families in the West and have always been for the people against all oppression. My action against Nimmo has nothing to do with politics.' Jim here unconsciously discloses what has been true of him all his life, that he has a kind of simplicity which makes him in both private and public politics lamentably stupid.

From the beginning of the General Strike there is difficulty, and it stems directly from the fundamentally opposing views of Chester and Jim: With an abhorrence of violence which goes back to the days of his earliest political activity recorded in *Except the Lord*, Chester will do all in his power to prevent fighting from breaking out. He will make deals; he will, as Jim says, wangle. But Jim will shoot, not because he loves violence but because he believes violence can both assert honour and restore order.

The climax comes when Jim suspects—correctly, as it

turns out—that Chester and the Communist leader Pin-comb have struck a secret bargain, "to sacrifice . . . the livelihood of three hundred families to the Bolshies in exchange for Bolshy support to Nimmo." Jim's man Maufe takes a truncheon to Pincomb, who is thereupon arrested—and tried for criminal assault. When Jim has a show-down with Chester, the old man is furious—and dishonest. Nina, who knows of Chester's machinations, throws herself under a lorry and is injured—how gravely, neither Chester nor Jim at first knows. While they are waiting for the report, Chester tells Jim: 'I am guilty before her and before you and before God. Whatever happens, I shall never see her again.' Thus Jim realizes, he records, why Nina has thrown herself under the lorry. "She could not pass that door into the lies inside, more wangles, more tricks. She was through with lies. I said in my heart, 'She had the truth in her soul—she was ready to die for it.'" This is as far as Jim can ever go.

As the book draws to a close, Jim's style becomes increasingly agitated, increasingly mad. Nina recovers. At the trial of Maufe she testifies tendentiously, but in such a way as to damn Maufe—when, in fact, as Jim later discovers, she is supporting Chester's position by suppressing evidence. To the reader of *Except the Lord* and *Prisoner of Grace*, her suppression is understandable. Fundamentally she trusts Chester's judgment. But to Jim, Nina's testimony is the ultimate evidence of betrayal. Justice has not been done to Maufe, but Jim intends that it shall be done to Nina and Chester. "Because of the rottenness. Because of the corruption. Because all loyalty was a laugh and there was no more trust."

After finishing the third volume of the political trilogy, the reader must ask himself once more about Chester Nimmo. Is he, as Nina asserts in *Prisoner of Grace*, "as good as he could be in his special circumstances, and better than many were in much easier ones"? Or is he, as he himself asserts in *Except the Lord* a man who "came so near perdition that his escape still seems to him like a miracle," but who has been saved by his lifelong devotion to the Protestant ideal, the Protestant faith in man's personal relationship to his God? Or is he, as Jim Latter asserts in *Not Honour More* simply a crook? To ask these questions is to reveal the complexity of the man, and the difficulty of arriving at an answer which will not do Chester the injustice of over-simplifying his personality and his achievement, or rather of underestimating his tragedy.

The answer must of course be in political terms. "What I believe," Cary wrote in a letter, "is what Nimmo believes, that wangle is inevitable in the modern state, that is to say, there is no choice between persuading people and shooting them. But it was not my job to state a thesis in a novel, my business was to show individual minds in action and the kind of world they produce and the political and aesthetic and moral problems of such a world. In short (in the trilogy), the political situation as I conceive it in *my* world of the creative free individual."

So Cary ends his great career as he began it, with the theme of freedom. The world of politics is his most difficult case, because politics is the most fluid of the arts. Yet Cary insists, in an article called "Political and Personal Morality," that "lies are always lies, evil is always evil; public and private morals are governed by precisely the same law. The destruction of one life by criminal pride or folly is no less and no more a crime than the slaughter of a million." "The world," Cary said in a broadcast ("Unfinished Novels"), "is not merely a flux of senseless change. Underneath all the turmoil there are certain fixed and permanent things too. In daily life there is always affection, family love and responsibility, ambition, the things people really live for; and on the other hand anxiety, loss, bitterness and danger, the everlasting dilemmas of life." Cary knew himself. He knew the world and despised it, but he knew life and relished it. Like the rest of his work the two trilogies are a presentation of life's magnificence, which leads not only to disaster, but also, because of man's freedom, to glory.

CARY'S PRELIMINARY NOTES ON
THE HORSE'S MOUTH
INCLUDING A REJECTED BEGINNING

(NOTE: *Words within square brackets are cancelled in the MS.; words within round brackets are doubtful readings; double round brackets indicate Joyce Cary's own parentheses; each asterisk indicates one illegible word or illegible fragmentary word.*)

Country is dead at the top. To foster the arts you must encourage the artist. You can't have material prosperity without that. Jimson grasps the function of Hickson but says not fulfilling it.

Jimson s book.

The Horse's Mouth

'I' is not an artist but [an official] a good chap suspicious of artists and no imagination but sentimental, good hearted vague

J. thinks of Sara s religion as 'a lightning conductor.' Brings everything round to evil herself. Cunningest piece of old shemale meat The old brisket. The heartful dodger.

Sees her forgive herself. Says, I'll own never bore resentment. [But even that was self indulgence.] didn't want to get wrinkles or spoil her fun. She used to say ** got his own back and the dog his vomit. She'd forgive the devil himself if he [were with was] had a spare seat for the fair.

She would do anything for anybody, especially herself J. says she dodged all responsibilities and got rid of furniture, pictures, even clothes.

J s version of her sending Tommy to school, to get him away because always playing about in the shed. ((Gulley doesn't want T. to be an artist.))

He sees Sara sent to police happiness as a *cats love of herself* and her comforts.

Jimson describes her cunning in passing the bad cheques [twice before] and nearly getting away to a place in Scotland

'You could push her over and have her and she would say no, no,

I won't, I won't. I mustn't.' and howl afterwards. and then she would be quite calm and say. It's no good crying over it, I suppose. I needn't spoil my eyes as well as my character

2 aspects of nature. Human nature. religious and sensual. rational and personal. Nature creative, forgetful, (producing) and renewing the fresh delight and (eye). Sara is tremendously impressed by her own luck, 'beyond her right,' and is sure she will be brought down 'No more than what I have to expect. She has intense enjoyment of life and appreciation of it as a boon. forgets her wrongs in enjoyment and activity. plans, cooking or amusement.

She thinks of others (nights) and pities them for their unhappiness and wonders at it.

She forgets griefs in new pleasures.

She forgets her sins and repentance and is surprised at herself—'a bad woman' and wonders how she loved and submitted to Matt.

———

With Jimson says never liked him but he liked me and [I liked] he was wonderfully gay and lively when he was in a good mood. [She enjoys] She enjoys his appreciation of her cooking and sensual pleasures and her body. Says she was too proud to run away. Wonderful what you can bear. and what is a (nose). Vanity. ((J. she howled and pitied her nose but forgot it all in ten minutes.))

She loves the place and makes herself cosy. and likes to see Jimson getting on. He paints more portraits and they spend money together ((J. says rows because she blued all the money. a fearfully extravagant woman in food and dress.))

Jimson says she caught him and ruined him. A study of the bourgeoise dame. Her questions, her vanity, her foolish mind, her corrupt flesh, her cunning ((all to exploit him)) he says". and yet she dominates him by her power and [because] flesh till [she] he is saved by the other woman, and returns to his real work, as he says, his abstractions. ((Doesn't know really whether they are nonsense or not. A blind creator.))

Saras book is full of her intense enjoyment of life and descriptions of people from, her point of view; [they] their success or failure in enjoyment of life. Wonder at their failure to enjoy.

Jimson's idea is that Wilcher Hickson and Sara want to exploit him [and] ((i.e., Corvo)). He writes them abusive letters. Describes how Sara used him ((? did she use him to express her vanity and W. to express her [mysticism] religion. Or as nature. Express her beauty through Jimson and her womans religious desire for [law and security and] sacrifice and service through Wilcher.)).

Rozzie says to J. of Sara. A devil for the men, [and] sucks em dry and leaves them for dead—and the way she's always on the rush. You look out, or she'll [kill] have you too and kill you. But J. takes up for cooking and as a model and she gets him—an awful life. I swore a dozen times I'd clear out but she got round me the same old way and then it all started again.'

[You] She saved you on models
'How do you (know)'
'Isn't that from her.'
'[What about] Yes, but you (ask) models and besides, she was old when I did that—[its] I say, you haven't seen anything else (from her).
'No, why.'
'Because (those) are the canvases that disappeared—*she* had em but she swears they were lost.'
'[But] Any girl then'
Jimson. '[(Just)] (Really) (just) [(shes)] life studies—nothing *in* them but I'd like to see em again.
((I think *life* studies is (quite) the (best)—they give you all the effect of a shot in the arm)).

[Having read two recent confessions books]
Last year two books were published [confessing] mentioning a man called Jimson, an artist who had some distinction about ten or fifteen years ago but is now forgotten. [But] [I thought] I [they reminded] knew Jimson thirty years ago. We were in Paris together, the old [Paris of the pre war] Paris of the Fauves, of 1910; and afterwards in London. I remembered him a noisy, dirty little man, always full of [art theories] new

theories of art and always taking up [new kinds of] a new style. (One moment) he would say Raphael was the only man and paint like an oleo lithograph; and the next he would be copying Van Gogh. [He did however settle down, *] (None) of [his] work was real; I mean it was all derived, mental stuff; [intended] (we) thought Jimson a faker; a chap who thought he could be [an artist] a great artist simply by taking to a [new style and painting hitting the public in the eye] queerer style than any body else and hitting the public in the eye with the biggest possible brush. He kidded himself, of course, as they all do, that he was a genius who worked in close collaboration with the Holy Spirit and that he hated the bourgeoise and so on; but [he] the truth was, he never forgot the (bourgeoise). His game too, as I say, was to make a big noise and [he hoped somehow to **] to do it by shocking his grandma.

There are, of course, two ways by which that kind of fake artist can make a big noise. He can go in for being a society painter, jib his way into the [*] academy, tickle the public in its soft spot, and make a pile and get a knighthood and all the rest of it. A good thing too. Society painters have their uses and some of their pictures are [(worth)] my most valuable possessions; that is, the National Gallery keeps them for me. Sargent, for instance, I wouldnt do without his ** for any money, if I had any money. They dont only make me laugh they bring back a whole period. Besides, I could kiss those Jewesses; holy Moses, what armfulls. Not meaning any disrespect to them or their race or their family.

Jimson could have been a Sargent if he had liked. He was a very accurate draughtsman; [*] with a wonderful eye for proportion; and he could slap on the colour [with as] better than any of us, in any style you liked. He was one of the most brilliant technicians I've ever seen; and we often told him he ought to go in for the fake market, painting Monets and [Vlamincs] Renoirs, and Corots and Ingres; [for the] even Rembrandts and Rubens; [to sell in the to the] for [dealers] the dealers in old masters. But this only made him angry. He was full of jokes but he never could take one about his art. That was a sore point. The reason was, of course, that down inside he knew damn well that he wasn't the real thing. He wasn't painting

159

because he had [to, but because] something to paint; but because he wanted to be a great man. Eaten up with ambition, poor devil.

[But of course since his] And since, by luck, he happened to have started [with me] in Paris, among us students who were all [for the new modern latest] agin the academies and salons, he thought that the only road to glory, [by was] otherwise noise, was by being agin the Sargents. [So he] and the [* and] academies too; and dying of [stra] starvation. So he painted terrible stuff and cursed the world.

[But a few years ago I saw a portrait about ten yea ten years ago I saw a thing]

I gave up painting as soon as I found I couldn't [paint. I had plenty to say but it wasn't the sort of thing] paint. [I didn't un] What I had been trying [to paint was ideas about things instead of instead of shapes and colours] to paint wasn't paintable: it was [music poetry and not even my own poe] only [pin] printable, or [if you] as it turned out, unprintable; so I went [into] on a newspaper and now I [am] keep an hotel. When I left Paris I lost touch with Jimson. I [(heard)] heard only that he was still being the unappreciated genius; still dirty and starving, [if possible]; and [I (saw)] still painting wonderful fakes. I saw [two] three of them; [portraits. One was] two portraits; an Orpen and a Modiliani; [I] and a wall, which was a take off of Stanley Spencer. But one day, a collector I know, a certain Mr. H. who has [the best eye I] a very fine taste, told me that Jimson had found himself, and he shewed me some photographs which made me sit up. I went to London specially to see the canvasses. They were all [piled up in] locked up in H s attic, piled up against a wall. He said that he had had a lot of trouble with Jimson about [payment the ownership] them and daren't show them in case Jimson tried to [blackmail him. He had his receipts but] put a knife through them. 'He's [lost all his facility painting q] capable of anything to get money, as you know and [he] although [he's been] he's been paid just what he asked for everything I have—and a great deal more for what he never delivered, he's trying to blackmail me for more. You know his method. He says his price was a thousand [indeed] and he's only had a hundred and if he's not paid, he'll take the thing back, or (cut it).'' I could well believe that Jimson [would (fly)] would play such a trick. He certainly liked money because he liked good living. [He would] But [*] an artist's (private) (duties) has nothing to do with his art and [this *] there was no doubt about the paintings. They were all first class, [real] the real thing; and they [all are off the same * (sprang) off the same mat] all belonged together. I [(never)] mean [to *] tho each was a real surprise, [like a new Picasso or a new as a (work) of] like a poem by a master, it [cast light] cast light on all the others. When you saw the lot, in a row; the effect was pretty [cousin] considerable. I don't say a row of Rembrandts or Titian's or even Goyas. [You can't] But I do say, a [real big man;] definite contribution and not a small one. The [grad] grand style. [Jimson Jimson] And Jimson's drawing, his great technique with paint, his energy and ambition, all the good qualities he had wasted; they were all there too. [It wa] Mind you, rather a noisy kind of effect. It was a brass band; but playing [on] something that could carry [the] brass.

'I congratulated Hickson and told him that he ought to get in touch with the Nat .Gall. Kenneth Clark, I said, is no mugwump, [and] he knows the big stuff, and he's ready to (chance) his (arm) for it. [These things] And things like this oughtn't to go out of the [country. *] country. [If the *] I can't imagine why the dealers haven't boosted him before, war or no war.'

Mr. Hickson said 'Because they haven't seen (them)'

'Do you mean this is the (lot)'

Yes, you may practically say that.

'All but a few [(wall) paintings and even they (can't) * hold a (candle)] ** [*] and they aren't in the same street as these. [You ***]

Jimson tells story of his life and dealings and pictures with especial account of women, the handmaids of the bawd. Nina Rozzie and Sara

Of Rozzie—get her out of the stays and she was just a female blancmange. All guts and no back bone. Rozzie's loyalty and straightness. Rozzie was a bit of the real old [dirt Devonshire] dirt—there was a lot of Queen Elizabeth [and (green) (victim) too] in Rozzie. I used to make prints on her bottom with the flat of my hand—came out [as blue] as clear as a drypoint—you could have photographed em for the *—and she used to jump nearly out of her skin and say Do that again and I'll knock your block off. [But she]* Go on, I like [it] a little attention.

She used to say, you're not a man you're a wasp. Well, I said, I've given you a nice little smelling, haven't I, and then she would say 'My God, [you are] I'm glad I'm not your wife— [your] poor Sara; and I would say 'What between you and Sara, I haven't touched a brush for a week'

And she would say 'What can I do now, and I would say 'Please yourself, old girl.' [*] My God, she would say, you ought to have your neck wrung, but I deserve it—I knew you were bad all through. (You), I said, you deserve it, and you've got it, old girl—you're in a bloody fine mess, aren't you. So she said 'It's not the baby, its the [money] cash, it'll cost me fifty pounds to get [out] rid of it—and I said to her '[By God] (Look here) Rozzie, no * fooling with the baby or I'll [* go to] cut your silly throat—that's my baby and its going to [live] be born or I'll know the reason why. I've never (hit) it off before [but I'm not (go)] and I'm not going to (lose my increase). [I tell you I I'll That G] You're going to have that baby and its going to be properly looked after, or [Holy] by the Holy Ho, I'll put the eye on you—[that means] the eye first and then the coppers. Why, I said, you damned old fool, that's what you want, a baby, it'll do you good. No, she said, I'm not that sort, I can't stand going [*] so soft—and all the mess too, [its] it'll get me down. And she was quite right too. [I had a fine time with her] Went all to pieces and I thought she'd die when her time came. She was forty five if a day. I believe she would have died but just at the worst, I came and said to her 'You die on me, you old bitch and I'll chase you into Hell and poke you [*] with your own damn frizzers.' I (wanted) her (milk), see—and it worked. She always responded to treatment and she nursed him too. [and] But she [never liked] got fond of him then. Yes, she got fond of him. The damned [(of)] old fool. Never was [*] such a baby. She used to sit and stare [smile] at him at an old parrot in the [zoo] zoo at a china egg. 'To think I did that' she'd say,' [It (expr) you] Who did it, I'd say, [Who do] That's my baby from the [first spit *] first [*], back belly and sides. Why, you old bag, I had to work at you like beating carpets. Well, she said, if you were a gentleman, you wouldn't say so. [Well,] so I said, I'm not a gentleman, I'm an [bloody (blasted arti)] artist, I'm a god, I make babies out of nothing. Out of me, you mean—says Rozzie. I said nothing. Well, said Rozzie, I hope there is a god to give you what you deserve. Not on your life, I said, I'll never be the king of the world. God doesn't give a fart for [*] me or you—he's up to his [games] own game. He's an artist, is God and he'll squeeze you out on his [canvas] palette any (morning) like a tube of [priming] flat white and throw the bladder in the ash can. Oh (yay), God is the [gorgeous chap] artist of the world. He's the glory of the stars—he's the man you (trim) you off an eye that beats Rubens.

((Give little bits of painting description))

J. sees her as unscrupulously arranging life to suit herself. i.e. turning Matts quiet religious household into a kind of brothel and nearly ruining him. Trying to exploit him and getting his pictures for nothing and selling them for hundreds. Says she had [a] hundreds in notes hidden away in the mattresses, especially after Rozzies death she sold to Hickson for 200 pounds. Then carrying off Wilcher [and] from under his family s nose and trying to carry him off too from Lizzie. Even took Tommy from him, and turned him into a little bourgeois such as cooks love.

First. Bellavista, the furniture, and the registry notice. Sara left to clean up.

(Everyone's) [(held) up &] go on but she likes place. Jimson frightens her. Worried about Gulley.

Rozzie and meeting with Gulley. Gulley and [(Billy) the *] the slummock and the boy. [Gulley * (appeal)] Gulley (appeals) to (her), [the (boy)] (then) (summons)—the boy. [the] Her (reminiscences)—and **. Two (sticks) of (Coal). Hicksons cheque and (salvage) rubbish.

(Day) for marriage, Mrs. Loftus comes in with a (police) and searches her box—finds [jewellery in * it] P.O. book and jewellery, for (sale). All comes out and she's astonished—(the stamps)—(taken) off in a cab to Police Station.

Gulley sends for her, ten pounds

Important points. *Description of the [p] Green.*
Tommy as a wild boy.
Gulley

W. says. She is exploited by everybody. J. says she exploits every one. Gave him ten pounds and bought the whole family. She loved to be in a buzz. (Just an) interest, and sex too, and marrying people. Sara (actually) loves work of organizing comfort and fun and happiness. [d] With Gulley, she improves shed, and the flat.

THE BLAKE QUOTATIONS IN
THE HORSE'S MOUTH

For the sake of verisimilitude—Gulley Jimson is dictating his memoirs—Blake's orthography is modernized by the author throughout *The Horse's Mouth*. In these notes, however, the Keynes text is followed.

Cary's glosses of certain of Blake's lines were undertaken in response to questions by the French translator of *The Horse's Mouth*.

ABBREVIATIONS:

Everyman: Max Plowman, ed., *The Poems & Prophecies of William Blake* (Everyman no. 792), London, Dent, 1927.

Keynes: Geoffrey Keynes, ed., *The Writings of William Blake*, 3 vols., London, Nonesuch, 1925.

S. & W.: D. J. Sloss and J. P. R. Wallis, *The Prophetic Writings of William Blake*, 2 vols., Oxford, Clarendon, 1926.

Carfax Edition
Page　　　　　*Catchwords or Full Quotation*

11 *"Five windows light . . ."*
"Europe: A Prophecy", lines 1-4: Everyman, p. 70; Keynes, I, 294; S. & W., I, 78.
(The lines omitted after *spheres* are:
". . . thro' one the eternal vine
Flourishes that he may recieve [*sic*] the grapes . . .")

28 *The pride of the peacock*
The Marriage of Heaven and Hell—"Proverbs of Hell", lines 23-25: Everyman, p. 45; Keynes, I, 185; S. & W., I, 15.

41 *"Because the soul of sweet delight . . ."*
"America: A Prophecy", lines 72-74: Everyman, p. 66; Keynes, I, 265; S. & W., I, 53.

("... *and polishes his door knob*" is Gulley's alteration. Blake's line reads:
"Amidst the lustful fire he walks; his feet become like brass,")

41 *For everything that lives is holy. Life delights in Life.*
"America: A Prophecy", line 71: Everyman, p. 65; Keynes, I, 265; S. & W., I, 53.
(These phrases also occur elsewhere in Blake's works. See "A Song of Liberty", last line: Everyman, p. 55; Keynes, I, 197; S. & W., I, 43. See also "Visions of the Daughters of Albion", line 215: Everyman, p. 62; Keynes, I, 261; S. & W., I, 39. See also *Vala, or the Four Zoas*, "Night the Second", line 574: Keynes, II, 34; S. & W., I, 187.)

41 *And every generated body*
"Milton"—Book the First, page 28, lines 31-36: Everyman, p. 140; Keynes, II, 345; S. & W., I, 400.
(Blake's line 33 reads:
Built by the Sons of Los in Bowlahoola & Allamanda:)
Cary's gloss of *In bright Cathedron's golden domes ...*: "In the realm of female creation giving the individual essences their particular essential existences, their 'generated bodies'."

42 *The world of imagination is the world of eternity.*
"A Vision of the Last Judgment", page 69: Everyman, p. 358; Keynes, III, 147; S. & W., II, 342.

43 *Life delights in Life.*
See second note to p. 41.

44 "*Ethinthus, queen of waters ...*"
"Europe: A Prophecy", lines 161-163: Everyman, p. 76; Keynes, I, 302; S. & W., I, 76.

48-71 *I travelled through a land of men*
The "*Pickering*" *MS.*—'The Mental Traveller", lines 1-4: Everyman, p. 325; Keynes, II, 223. (Since this poem is so important in this section of *The Horse's Mouth*, I print it in full below.)

THE BLAKE QUOTATIONS
The Mental Traveller

I travel'd thro' a Land of Men,
A Land of Men & Women too,
And heard & saw such dreadful things
As cold Earth wanderers never knew.

For there the Babe is born in joy
That was begotten in dire woe;
Just as we Reap in joy the fruit
Which we in bitter tears did sow.

And if the Babe is born a Boy
He's given to a Woman Old,
Who nails him down upon a rock,
Catches his shrieks in cups of gold.

She binds iron thorns around his head,
She pierces both his hands & feet,
She cuts his heart out at his side
To make it feel both cold & heat.

Her fingers number every Nerve,
Just as a Miser counts his gold;
She lives upon his shrieks & cries,
And she grows young as he grows old.

Till he becomes a bleeding youth,
And she becomes a Virgin bright;
Then he rends up his Manacles
And binds her down for his delight.

He plants himself in all her Nerves,
Just as a Husbandman his mould;
And she becomes his dwelling place
And Garden fruitful seventy fold.

An aged Shadow, soon he fades,
Wand'ring round an Earthly Cot,
Full filled all with gems & gold
Which he by industry had got.

And these are the gems of the Human Soul,
The rubies & pearls of a lovesick eye,
The countless gold of the akeing heart,
The martyr's groan & the lover's sigh.

They are his meat, they are his drink;
He feeds the Beggar & the Poor
And the wayfaring Traveller:
For ever open is his door.

His grief is their eternal joy;
They make the roofs & walls to ring;
Till from the fire on the hearth
A little Female Babe does spring.

And she is all of solid fire
And gems & gold, that none his hand
Dares stretch to touch her Baby form,
Or wrap her in his swaddling band.

But she comes to the Man she loves,
If young or old, or rich or poor;
They soon drive out the aged Host,
A Beggar at another's door.

He wanders weeping far away,
Until some other take him in;
Oft blind & age-bent, sore distrest,
Untill he can a Maiden win.

And to allay his freezing Age
The Poor Man takes her in his arms;
The cottage fades before his sight,
The Garden & its lovely Charms.

The Guests are scatter'd thro' the land,
For the Eye altering alters all;
The Senses roll themselves in fear,
And the flat Earth becomes a Ball;

THE BLAKE QUOTATIONS

The stars, sun, Moon, all shrink away,
A desart vast without a bound,
And nothing left to eat or drink,
And a dark desart all around.

The honey of her Infant lips
The bread & wine of her sweet smile,
The wild game of her roving Eye,
Does him to Infancy beguile;

For as he eats & drinks he grows
Younger & younger every day;
And on the desart wild they both
Wander in terror & dismay.

Like the Stag she flees away,
Her fear plants many a thicket wild;
While he pursues her night & day,
In various arts of Love beguil'd,

By various arts of Love & Hate,
Till the wide desart planted O'er
With Labyrinths of wayward Love,
Where roam the Lion, Wolf, & Boar,

Till he becomes a wayward Babe,
And she a weeping Woman Old.
Then many a Lover wanders here;
The Sun & Stars are nearer roll'd.

The trees bring forth sweet Extacy
To all who in the desart roam;
Till many a City there is Built,
And many a pleasant Shepherd's home.

But when they find the frowning Babe,
Terror strikes thro' the region wide:
They cry "The Babe! the Babe is Born!"
And flee away on Every side.

For who dare touch the frowning form,
His arm is wither'd to its root;
Lions, Boars, Wolves, all howling flee,
And every Tree does shed its fruit.

And none can touch that frowning form,
Except it be a Woman Old;
She nails him down upon a Rock,
And all is done as I have told.

Page   *Catchwords or Full Quotation*

84 *Till we have built Jerusalem*
"Milton"—Preface: Everyman, p. 109; Keynes, II, 306;
S. & W., I, 356.

89 *These lovely females form sweet night*
"Milton"—Book the First, page 25, lines 39, 40: Everyman, p. 135; Keynes, II, 339; S. & W., I, 389.

93 *And this is the manner*
"Milton"—Book the First, lines 5-10: Everyman, p. 113; Keynes, II, 310; S. & W., I, 430.

97 *For Eternity is in love with the productions of time*
The Marriage of Heaven and Hell—"Proverbs of Hell", line 10: Everyman, p. 45; Keynes, I, 184; S. & W., I, 15.

99 *And the Sons of Los*
"Milton"—Book the First, page 30, lines 44-46, 48-50, 62, 63; page 31, line 1: Everyman, pp. 143, 144; Keynes, II, 349; S. & W., I, 402, 403.
(Blake's line 47 reads:
(*A moment equals a pulsation of the artery*),)

100 *And every space*
"Milton"—Book the First, page 31, lines 21, 22: Everyman, p. 144; Keynes, II, 350; S. & W., I, 405.

104 *Oothoon wandered in woe*
"Visions of the Daughters of Albion", lines 3-7: Everyman, p. 56; Keynes, I, 254; S. & W., I, 31.

105 *The golden nymph replied . . .*
"Visions of the Daughters of Albion", line 8: Everyman, p. 56; Keynes, I, 254; S. & W., I, 31.

Cary's gloss of the last two lines: "What Blake means is 'giving to airy nothing a delightful name with bounds belonging to eternal forms'. For Blake every individual character had its own nature, its 'particular' shape, rather like a Platonic form. This was its essentiality by which it

171

was eternal and belonged to the realm of the 'infinite'.
'Bounds *to* the infinite' reads like a contradiction in terms
but one can follow the thought. Translate 'bounds in the
eternal reality or form of the real'. You are you, and
nobody else. Anything 'real' or partaking of eternal form,
beauty, goodness etc. depends therefore on your individual
difference."

154 *Tiger, tiger, burning bright*
Songs of Experience—"The Tyger": Everyman, p. 28;
Keynes, I, 284.

155 *Where every female delights . . .*
"Jerusalem"—Chapter III, page 69, lines 15-18: Everyman, p. 246; Keynes, III, 272; S. & W., I, 579.

155 *Fearful Symmetry*
Songs of Experience—"The Tyger": Everyman, p. 28;
Keynes, I, 284.

156 *She Creates at her will*
"Jerusalem"—Chapter III, page 69, lines 19-22: Everyman, p. 246; Keynes, III, 272; S. & W., I, 579.

157 *And every moment*
"Milton"—Book the First, page 30, lines 46; 48-50:
Everyman, p. 143; Keynes, II, 349; S. & W., I, 402.
(Blake's line 47 reads:
(*A Moment equals a pulsation of the artery*),)

178 *Ulro*
Cary's gloss: "the vegetative, materialistic state of the
soul".

186 *But all within is opened*
"Jerusalem"—Chapter I, page 5, lines 56-58: Everyman,
p. 166; Keynes, III, 171; S. & W., I, 452.

220 *A Satan in a mill*
The phrases "mills of Satan" and "Satanic mills" occur
many times in "Milton".

220 *"I also stood in Satan's bosom . . ."*
"Milton"—Book the Second, page 43, lines 15-21: Everyman, p. 156; Keynes, II, 365; S. & W., I, 419.

THE BLAKE QUOTATIONS

BIBLIOGRAPHY

1 *Novels*

All but the last two of the novels have been published in the Carfax edition, which, with one exception, is to be preferred because each volume contains a preface specially written by Cary. The exception is *The Horse's Mouth*, of which an authoritative text was published in 1957, together with illustrations by Cary, the Carfax preface, "The Old Strife at Plant's" (a discarded chapter of *The Horse's Mouth*), identification of the Blake quotations, and bibliography.

Aissa Saved. London, Ernest Benn, 1932; London, Michael Joseph, 1949; London, Michael Joseph (Carfax edition), 1952.

An American Visitor. London, Ernest Benn, 1933; London, Michael Joseph, 1949; London, Michael Joseph (Carfax edition), 1952.

The African Witch. London, Victor Gollancz, 1936: Book Society Choice; New York, William Morrow, 1936; London, Michael Joseph, 1950; London, Michael Joseph (Carfax edition), 1951.

Castle Corner. London, Victor Gollancz, 1938: Book Society Recommendation; London, Michael Joseph, 1950; London, Michael Joseph (Carfax edition), 1952.

Mister Johnson. London, Victor Gollancz, 1939; London, Michael Joseph, 1947; New York, Harper, 1951; London, Michael Joseph (Carfax edition), 1952.

Charley is My Darling. London, Michael Joseph, 1940: Book Society Recommendation; London, Michael Joseph (Carfax edition), 1951.

A House of Children. London, Michael Joseph, 1941: Awarded the James Tait Black Memorial Prize, 1941; London, Michael Joseph (Carfax edition), 1951; Harmondsworth, Penguin Books, 1955; New York, Harper, 1956; Vienna, Guild Books, n.d.

Herself Surprised. London, Michael Joseph, 1941; New York, Harper, 1948; London, Michael Joseph (Carfax edition),

1951; Harmondsworth, Penguin Books, 1955; New York, Dell, n.d. (*ca.* 1955).

To be a Pilgrim. London, Michael Joseph, 1942; New York, Harper, 1949; London, Michael Joseph (Carfax edition), 1951; Harmondsworth, Penguin Books, 1957.

The Horse's Mouth. London, Michael Joseph, 1944: Book Society Recommendation; Harmondsworth, Penguin Books, 1948; London, Readers Union, 1945; New York, Harper, 1950: Book-of-the-Month Club Selection for January 1950; London, Michael Joseph (Carfax edition), 1951; London, George Rainbird in association with Michael Joseph, 1957, edited by Andrew Wright.

First Trilogy. New York, Harper, 1958.

The Moonlight. London, Michael Joseph, 1946: Book Society Recommendation; New York, Harper, 1947; London, Michael Joseph (Carfax edition), 1952.

A Fearful Joy. London, Michael Joseph, 1949; New York, Harper, 1950; London, Michael Joseph (Carfax edition), 1952; Harmondsworth, Penguin Books, 1956 (dated in error 1955).

Prisoner of Grace. London, Michael Joseph, 1952; New York, Harper, 1952; London, Michael Joseph (Carfax edition), 1954; London, Readers Union, 1954.

Except the Lord. London, Michael Joseph, 1953; New York, Harper, 1953.

Not Honour More. London, Michael Joseph, 1955; New York, Harper, 1955.

2 Short Fiction

Babes in the Wood. *Evening News*, May 28, 1953, p. 9.

The Bad Samaritan. (pseud. Thomas Joyce) *Saturday Evening Post*, July 3, 1920, pp. 40–46.

The Breakout. *New Yorker*, February 2, 1957, pp. 28–36.

Bush River. *Windmill*, I (1945), 120–125.

Buying a Horse. *Punch*, December 2, 1953, pp. 654–656.

Carmagnole. *London Magazine*, II (February 1955), 37–39.

A Consistent Woman. (pseud. Thomas Joyce) *Saturday Evening Post*, August 21, 1920, pp. 30, 32, 81, 82.

The Cure (pseud. Thomas Joyce) *Saturday Evening Post*, May 1, 1920, pp. 30, 99.

JOYCE CARY

A Date. (also called "Red Letter Day") *New Yorker*, August 1, 1953, pp. 56-58; *Punch*, October 21, 1953, pp. 478-480.

Dinner at the Beeders'. (excerpt of *The Horse's Mouth*) *Harper's*, CXCIX (September 1949), 38-46.

Evangelist. *Harper's*, CCV (November 1952), 88, 89; (U.K.) *Harper's Bazaar*, (May 1954), 68, 69.

A Glory of the Moon. *Mademoiselle*, XLI (May 1955), 101, 156.

A Good Investment. *Harper's*, CCIX (December 1954), 64-72.

Growing Up. (U.S.) *Vogue*, May 1, 1956, pp. 122, 123, 160.

Happy Marriage. *Harper's*, CCXVI (April 1958), 65-68.

A Hot Day. *Time and Tide*, June 16, 1956, p. 710.

The Idealist. (pseud. Thomas Joyce) *Saturday Evening Post*, March 13, 1920, pp. 40-42.

Jubilee Christmas. *Mademoiselle*, XLII (December 1955), 62, 63.

The Limit. *Esquire*, XLI (June 1954), 43.

Lombrosine. (pseud. Thomas Joyce) *Saturday Evening Post*, January 31, 1920, pp. 30, 32, 62.

A Mysterious Affair. *New Yorker*, January 28, 1956, pp. 28-34.

None but the Brave. (pseud. Thomas Joyce) *Saturday Evening Post*, September 11, 1920, pp. 18, 19, 100, 104, 107, 110.

The Old Strife at Plant's. (a discarded chapter of *The Horse's Mouth*), *Harper's*, CCI (August 1950), 80-96; Oxford, privately printed with illustrations by the author, 1956.

Out of Hand. (U.S.) *Vogue*, CXXVI (July 1955), 60-62.

Period Piece. (U.S.) *Harper's Bazaar* (April 1958), 110, 111, 208.

A Piece of Honesty. (pseud. Thomas Joyce) *Saturday Evening Post*, June 26, 1920, pp. 66, 69, 70.

A Private Ghost. *New Yorker*, November 10, 1956, pp. 121-130.

Psychologist. (U.S.) *Harper's Bazaar*, XC (May 1957), 140-142, 175-185.

Red Letter Day. See under "A Date".

The Reformation. (pseud. Thomas Joyce) *Saturday Evening Post*, May 22, 1920, pp. 20, 21, 124.

Romance. *Time*, October 20, 1952, p. 119.

Salute to Propriety. (pseud. Thomas Joyce) *Saturday Evening Post*, October 9, 1920, pp. 40, 42, 45, 46.

A Special Occasion. *Harper's*, CCIII (September 1951), 97-98; *Cornhill*, CLXV (Winter 1951-1952), 387-389.

BIBLIOGRAPHY

Spring Song. *London Magazine,* I (March 1954), 29-31.
The Springs of Youth. (pseud. Thomas Joyce) *Saturday Evening Post,* March 6, 1920, pp. 30, 32, 189, 190.
Success Story. *Harper's,* CCIV (June 1952), 74-76.
The Tunnel. (U.S.) *Vogue,* October 1, 1957, pp. 186, 187, 226.
Umaru. *Cornhill,* CLXV (Winter 1950-1951), 50-54.
You're Only Young Once. *Encounter,* VIII (September 1956), 24-26.

3 Political Treatises

Power in Men. London, Nicholson and Watson (for the Liberal Book Club), 1939.
The Case for African Freedom. London, Secker and Warburg, 1941; revised and enlarged edition, 1944.
Process of Real Freedom. London, Michael Joseph, 1943.
Britain and West Africa. London, Longmans, Green, 1946; revised edition, 1947.

4 Poems

A Lawn, and in the Midst a Silken Pool. (published anonymously) *The Cliftonian,* XIX (June 1906), 194, 195.
Verse. (by Arthur Cary: "Arthur" is Joyce Cary's first Christian name) Edinburgh, Robert Grant, 1908.
I Watched Blind Planets Weave Their Chains. *Modern Reading No. 13,* ed. Reginald Moore, London, Wells, Gardner, Darton, 1945, p. 19.
Marching Soldier. London, Michael Joseph, 1945.
The Drunken Sailor: A Ballad-Epic. London, Michael Joseph, 1947.

5 Essays in Criticism

L'Art. *New York Times Book Review,* March 12, 1950, p. 8.
Art and Reality. (The Clark Lectures 1956) Cambridge, Cambridge University Press; New York, Harper, 1958.
Catching up with History. (a review of Richard Wright's *Black Power*) *Nation,* October 16, 1954, pp. 332, 333.
[On Censorship]. *Author,* LXII (1952), 84, 85.

177

The Censorship Plot. *Spectator*, March 11, 1955, pp. 275, 276.
Character on the Manhattan Boat. *New York Times Book Review*, June 6, 1954, p. 2.
[On *The Decameron*]. *The Times*, August 2, 1954, p. 7.
On the Function of the Novelist. *New York Times Book Review*, October 30, 1949, pp. 1, 52.
Gerald Wilde. *Nimbus*, III, ii (1955), 47-54.
Horror Comics. *Spectator*, February 18, 1955, p. 177.
Important Authors of the Fall, Speaking for Themselves. *New York Herald-Tribune Book Review*, October 8, 1950, p. 10.
Including Mr. Micawber. *New York Times Book Review*, April 15, 1951, p. 4.
[An Interview with Joyce Cary]. (conducted by John Burrows and Alex Hamilton) *Paris Review*, VIII (Winter 1954-1955), 63-78. Reprinted in Malcolm Cowley, ed., *Writers at Work: The Paris Review Interviews*. New York, Viking, 1958, pp. 51-67.
My First Novel. *Listener*, April 16, 1953, pp. 637, 638.
Notes sur l'art et la liberté. (translated by A. Proudhommeaux) *Preuves*, XLII (August 1954), 28-32.
A Novel is a Novel is a Novel. *New York Times Book Review*, April 30, 1950, pp. 1, 34.
A Novelist and His Public. *Listener*, September 30, 1954, pp. 521, 522; *Saturday Review*, November 27, 1954, pp. 11, 36, 37.
The Novelist at Work: A Conversation between Joyce Cary and Lord David Cecil. *Adam International Review*, XVIII, nos. 212-213 (November-December 1950), 15-25.
Party of One. *Holiday*, XX (September 1956), 6, 89.
The Period Novel. *Spectator*, November 21, 1952, p. 684.
The Revolution of the Women. (U.S.) *Vogue*, March 15, 1951, pp. 99, 100, 149.
Roman à Thèse. (translated by Christine Lalou) *Nouvelles Littéraires*, August 11, 1955, pp. 1, 2.
A Slight Case of Demolition. *Sunday Times*, May 20, 1956, p. 6.
Speaking of Books. *New York Times Book Review*, June 26, 1955, p. 2.
Tolstoy's Theory of Art. *University of Edinburgh Journal*, XII (Summer 1943), 91-96.

BIBLIOGRAPHY

The Way a Novel Gets Written. *Harper's*, CC (February 1950), 87-93.

What Does Art Create? *Literature and Life*, II, Addresses to the English Association by Margaret Willy, *et al.*, London, Harrap, 1951, pp. 32-45.

6 *Other Essays*

Africa Yesterday: One Ruler's Burden. *Reporter*, May 15, 1951, pp. 21-24.

Barney Magonagel. *New Yorker*, June 19, 1954, pp. 27-31.

Britain is Strong in Herself. *New York Times Magazine*, April 22, 1956, pp. 12, 32, 33.

Can Western Values Survive without Religion? *Time and Tide*, July 9, 1955, pp. 901, 902 (the second part of this essay, called "Faith in Liberty", appears in the issue of July 16, 1955, pp. 933, 934).

A Child's Religion. (U.S.) *Vogue*, CXXII (December 1953), 86, 87.

Christmas in Africa. *Esquire*, XL (December 1953), 101, 208.

Cromwell House. *New Yorker*, November 3, 1956, pp. 45-67.

Faith in Liberty. See under "Can Western Values Survive without Religion?"

The Front-Line Feeling. *Listener*, January 17, 1952, pp. 92, 93.

The Heart of England. *Holiday*, XVII (January 1955), 26-31.

The Idea of Progress. (also called "Is the World Getting Anywhere?"), *Cornhill*, CLXVII (Summer 1954), 331-337; (U.S.) *Vogue*, March 15, 1954, pp. 68-71.

L'Influence britannique dans la révolution libérale. (translated by M. Bouvier) *Comprendre*, nos. 13-14 (June 1955), 45-51.

Is the World Getting Anywhere? See under "The Idea of Progress".

Joyce Cary's Last Look at His Worlds. (U.S.) *Vogue*, August 15, 1957, pp. 96, 97, 150-153.

[A Letter to *The Listener* on Religion]. *Listener*, January 12, 1956, p. 65.

Look Out for Labels. *This Week Magazine*, January 4, 1953, p. 2.

179

The Mass Mind: Our Favorite Folly. (also called "Mass Mind: A Modern Catch-Word" and "Myth of the Mass Mind") *Harper's,* CCIV (March 1952), 25-27; *Cornhill,* CLXVI (Summer 1952), 138-142; *Readers Digest,* LXII (February 1953), 135, 136.

The Meaning of England. *Holiday,* XXIII (April 1958), 117.

The Most Exciting Sport in the World. *Holiday,* XXI (June 1957), 42-48; 155-157.

Oxford Scholar. *Holiday,* XIII (June 1953), 96-101.

Party of One. *Holiday,* XVI (November 1954), 6, 8, 11, 12, 97.

Personality [A. P. Herbert]. (published anonymously) *Time,* March 10, 1952, p. 45.

Policy for Aid. *Confluence,* IV (1955), 292-301.

Political and Personal Morality. *Saturday Review,* December 31, 1955, pp. 5, 6, 31, 32.

Proposals for Peace—III. *Nation,* January 10, 1953, p. 28.

The Sources of Tension in America. *Saturday Review,* August 23, 1952, pp. 6, 7, 35.

Switzerland. *Holiday,* XVI (August 1954), 27-37.

Westminster Abbey. *Holiday,* XIX (April 1956), 62, 63.

Why They Say 'God Save the Queen'. *New York Times Magazine,* May 31, 1953, p. 7.

7 *Some Important Secondary Sources*

—. Cheerful Protestant. *Time,* October 20, 1952, pp. 118-130.

Adam International Review, XVIII, nos. 212-213 (November-December 1950). Issue devoted to Joyce Cary.

Allen, Walter Ernest. Joyce Cary. (Bibliographical Series of Supplements to *British Book News*) London, Longmans, Green, 1953.

Bettman, Elizabeth R. Joyce Cary and the Problem of Political Morality. *Antioch Review,* XVII (1957), 266-272.

Bowen, Elizabeth. An Old Chap. *Tatler,* November 4, 1942, p. 152.

Case, Edward. In the Great Tradition. *Wall Street Journal,* June 6, 1955, p. 10.

Collins, Harold R. Joyce Cary's Troublesome Africans. *Antioch Review,* XIII (1953), 397-406.

BIBLIOGRAPHY

Craig, David. Idea and Imagination: A Study of Joyce Cary. *Fox* (published by Aberdeen University Classical, Literary, and Philosophical Societies), n.d. (*ca.* 1954), pp. 3-10.

Hardy, Barbara. Form in Joyce Cary's Novels. *Essays in Criticism*, IV (1954), 180-190.

Hatfield, Glenn W., Jr. Form and Character in the Sequence Novels of Joyce Cary. Thesis (unpublished), Ohio State University, 1956.

Hayes, Richard. Felt in the Head and Felt along the Heart. *Commonweal*, October 17, 1952, p. 42.

Hicks, Granville. Living with Books. *New Leader*, June 13, 1955, pp. 21, 22.

Hughes, Richard. Joyce Cary. *Spectator*, December 18, 1953, pp. 738, 739.

Johnson, Pamela Hansford. Three Novelists and the Drawing of Character: C. P. Snow, Joyce Cary, and Ivy Compton-Burnett. *Essays and Studies by Members of the English Association*, N.S. III (1950), 82-91.

Jones, Ernest. The Double View. *Nation*, February 25, 1950, pp. 184-186.

Kettle, Arnold [On *Mister Johnson*]. *An Introduction to the English Novel*, II, London, Hutchinson's Home University Library, 1953, pp. 177-184.

[Maclaren Ross, Julian]. Story of a Full Life. *Times Literary Supplement*, November 11, 1949, p. 732.

Monas, Sidney. What to Do With a Drunken Sailor. *Hudson Review*, III (1950), 466-474.

Murry, John Middleton. Coming to London. *London Magazine*, III (July 1956), 30-37.

Prescott, Orville. Two Modern Masters: Cozzens, Cary. *In My Opinion*. Indianapolis, Bobbs-Merrill, 1952, pp. 180-199.

Pritchett, Victor S. Books in General. *New Statesman and Nation*, October 27, 1951, pp. 464, 465.

Rosenfeld, Isaac. Popular Misery. *New Republic*, October 20, 1952, p. 27.

Van Horn, Ruth G. Freedom and Imagination in the Novels of Joyce Cary. *Midwest Journal*, V (1952-1953), 19-30.

Woodcock, George. Citizens of Babel: A Study of Joyce Cary. *Queens Quarterly*, LXIII (1956), 236-246.

Index

183

JOYCE CARY

Cary, Joyce—(*contd.*)
House of Children—7; 17-19;
31, 32; 62-65; 73; 75, 76;
88-90; 97; 103; 107; 108, 109;
"L'Influence britannique dans
la révolution libérale"—39;
*The King is Dead, Long Live the
King*—56, 57; "A Lawn, and
in the Midst a Silken Pool"—
20; life — 16-27; *Marching
Soldier* — 42-44; *Markby*—49,
50; *Marta*—50; 52-54; *Memoir
of the Bobotes*—24; *Men of
Two Worlds*—27; *Mister Johnson*—15; 36; 38; 46; 57, 58; 61,
62; 66; 76; 84-87; 92; 96, 97;
The Moonlight—31; 32; 67-69;
70; 76; 77; 90; 92; 97; 98; 103,
104; 105; "My First Novel"—
14; 57, 58; *Not Honour More*—
15; 36, 37; 43; 53; 74; 76; 93;
94; 97; 138; 148-153; 154;
"The Old Strife at Plant's"—
14; 130, 131; originality—13,
14; permission to write about
him—7, 8; poetry—41-45;
point of view in the novels—
13, 14; 15, 16; 76, 77; 109,
110; 153-155; "Political and
Personal Morality" — 154;
political writings—34-41; 150;
154; *Power in Men*—34-37;
Prisoner of Grace—15; 43; 53; 61;
67; 73; 76; 90; 97; 98; 105, 106;
137-142; 150; 153; 154; *Process of Real Freedom*—35; 41;
"Roman à Thèse"—31; 40;
46; 70; "Romance" — 47;
short stories—11; 25; 45-49;
"A Special Occasion"—46,
47; "Spring Song" — 48;
"Success Story" — 48, 49;
theme of the novels—15, 16;
28-71; 154, 155; *To be a
Pilgrim*—15; 72; 73; 74; 76,
77; 92; 93; 94; 97; 109, 110;
119-124; *To Sleep in Ulro*—50;
Todd — 50; *Tottenham* — 50;

"Umaru" — 46; "Unfinished
Novels"—154, 155; unpub-
lished work—11, 12; 14; 23;
24; 26; 42; 49-57; *Verse*—41,
42; "The Way a Novel Gets
Written"—118; *William*—49,
50.
Cary, Michael. Son of J. C.—25
Cary, Peter. Son of J. C.—25
Cary, Tristram. Son of J. C.—25
Cary, Tristram. Uncle of J. C.
—19
Castro, Américo. On *Lazarillo de
Tormes*—111
Chandler, Arnold. Bibliographer
—9
Chaucer, Geoffrey. Wife of Bath
—112
Coleridge, Samuel Taylor. In-
fluence in *The Drunken Sailor*—
44
Conrad, Joseph. "Heart of Dark-
ness"—31; 73; imitated by
J. C.—26; modernity—30;
narrative management — 13;
one of J. C.'s masters—58
Corvo, Frederick Baron (i.e.,
Frederick Rolfe). Model for
Gulley Jimson—158
Craig, David. Critic of J. C.—9
Crane, Stephen. Deterministic
notions — 36; "The Open
Boat"—36

Davin, Anna. Friend of J. C.
—9
Davin, Dan. Friend of J. C.—9
Davin, Winifred. Friend of J. C.
—9
Defoe, Daniel. *Moll Flanders*—
29; 111, 112; naturalness and
zest—28
Dickens, Charles. Characterization—29; comic lavishness—
—111; *Hard Times*—30; tag
names—13
Dorsey, Clarene. Bibliographer
—9

INDEX

185